Blooming Rose

Just For Today…

Healing Words for a Woman's Heart

Copyright © Gaia Rose
2018 Re-edition

All rights reserved, including the right to reproduce this book, or portions thereof in any form. No part of this text may be reproduced, transmitted, downloaded, decompiled, reverse engineered, or stored, in any form or introduced into any information storage and retrieval system, in any form or by any means, whether electronic or mechanical without the express written permission of the author.

The views expressed in this work are solely those of the author.

ISBN; 978-0-244-06591-1

I dedicate this book to all women of the world.

You are never alone.

Acknowledgments

To each and every soul who has been part of my journey so far.

To my passion, who without I wouldn't have the inner fire to create.

To my pain, who pushes me to grow.

To Mother Earth who keeps me grounded in my feminine Nature.

To my heart, who has and will always be my greatest teacher, helping me stay true to my unique essence - for myself, and for those around me.

Thank you all.

Introduction

Sometimes we women need an ear to listen or simply an encouraging word, but too often than not the times we need this comfort the most is the exact time we pull back, hide away, and feel less comfortable with asking for help. As a woman myself I have at many times wanted some words of empowerment or guidance, but held back from asking in fear of looking weak of exposing my vulnerability. Although I'm much more comfortable with being open and raw now when I'm in my shadow of emotions, I still at times withdraw (albeit very few times) and in those times of hiding I often reach for a book to find some light of hope, a different way of looking at things, or some words of wisdom and guidance to help me feel not so alone in my thoughts and feelings.

When I chose to write *The Blossoming Rose* I wrote it with that exact intention in my heart; to help offer a little pocket book of guidance and empowerment to women in those times of struggle and withdrawal.

The truth is not all of us are blessed to have another caring soul to share our heart with, and as a passionate writer I believe that in these circumstances books can come in and offer hope to those who may find it difficult to ask.

Through my early childhood years of sexual and physical abuse, the loss of my baby sister, homelessness as a teenager, drug and alcohol addiction, then losing my big brother Michael at the age of 24, I think it's fair to say there were many times I gave up, withdrew from it all, didn't know which way to turn, and deeply struggled with asking for help. At this time of utter loneliness, I began my inner journey back to self. I would read many books, just like this one you hold in your hand, and although I didn't fully realise it at the time, in hindsight it was by diving deeply into books which was actually part of what helped me to rise more, whilst feeling a greater connection to myself, my heart, my pain, and to those around me.

In many ways I guess you could say that why I became an author was because I knew how powerful and inspiring words could be for another when written from the heart. Although I have been a writer all of my life through poetry and song, which greatly helped me express myself in a very healing way, it wasn't until the loss of my brother and reading all the many self-help books I did, that my journey as an author came to life.

My prayer for you is that through this little book you hold in your hands you will find comfort, healing, empowerment, and a sense of connection, knowing that you are never alone in your struggles and that there is always hope, as long as you never stop believing in yourself.

So, go forth with an open heart and may the messages in this book help you re-connect with your inner Goddess, your true Feminine essence, your beauty, and the greatness within, so you may walk this

Earth continuing to blossom into the beautiful rose you were born to be!

Gaia Rose

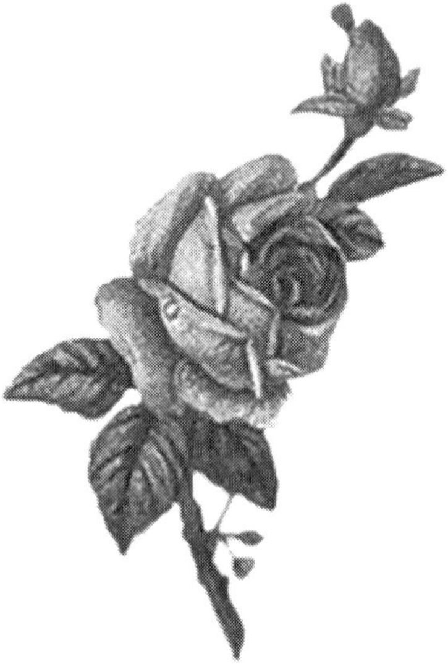

Woman, You Are Free To Be Wild

Woman, you're free to be Wild!...to Empower the Goddess and Unleash the Wolf roaring within your womb, howling to be released.

Woman, you're free to be Wild!...to defend, to assert, to express, and to say it as your own feminine heart chooses.

Woman, you're free to be Wild!...to rise and fall, to stumble, to not be so bloody perfect, to drop the mask and show Her to the world.

Woman, you're free to be Wild!...to let 'crazy' out once in a while, to scream, to voice, to speak up and release all Her fire of passion that's burning beneath.

Woman, you're free to be Wild!...to be untamed, to say no, to say yes, to break rules and create your own, to do it your own unique way – the way She is calling you to, and to see how life flows best for you.

Woman, you're free to be Wild!...to be unchained from societal conditioning, to be different, to stand alone, to be feared, and to be the lone wolf.

Woman, you're free to be Wild!...to be sexy, sensual, and confident with every inch of your curves, to be attractive, to own your beauty, to move your hips, to dance, to sing, to raise your arms, to lift your pelvis, to arch your back, and to surrender.

Woman, you're free to be Wild!...to demand respect, honour, value, and truth, to stand your ground, to raise your standards, to know your worth, to call out the bulls**t, and to walk away from anyone who doesn't honour this.

Woman, you're free to be Wild!...to feel, to love, to create, to birth, to experience, to walk bear foot upon Mother Gaia, to swim naked in the rivers, to share, to receive, and to change path at any given moment.

Woman, you're free to be Wild!...to Be you, to See you, to Feel you, and to love the crap out of all you were, all you are, all who you're going to be, and everything which makes your own feminine heart come alive the most!

Woman, you're free to be Wild!
So why am I still reminding you?

JUST FOR TODAY...

Pray

You don't have to be religious to pray, you don't have to go to church, have certain beliefs, or believe in a God, all you need is an open mind and an open heart. It's truly an amazing feeling when we ask the universe for help, talk about our struggles, pray for another soul or confess our sins etc. Personally, I find it better when talking out loud (if possible), rather than just in my mind, but as long as you're speaking from your heart and a place of truth, either way works fine.

Praying shifts something deep inside of our being. The energy of every thought and every feeling that we've been holding onto gets released, helping to slowly move our unwanted energy out into the universe and away from us, as energy cannot be destroyed, only transferred. This is all praying really is - directing and releasing unwanted energy into a safe space where it can be turned into something beautiful, rather than holding it in our hearts or directing it onto a person where it could do more harm than good.

You may even wish to pray for all you're grateful for. The most beautiful of prayers are those full of thankfulness.

If you find you're feeling unsettled in any way, first take note of the feeling, then you'll understand where the thoughts are arising from. Once you are in your heart, take a moment to literally kneel down and pray. Imagine you're talking to a friend, you don't need to prepare, just allow yourself to *be* and surrender to what comes out. Doing it this way, from your heart, will always reveal the greatest truth which will then help you to receive the answers you've been searching for.

JUST FOR TODAY...

Know You Are A Sensual Spirit

Yes, you *are* aloud to feel beautiful!

Don't push away your sensuality…it's part of what makes you woman. We can *all* follow a spiritual path and still keep in touch with our sensual sexy side (no matter what society may say). It's enormously empowering when we women learn to accept our body, connect *without* just as much as we do *within* and be proud of our womanly prowess, be proud of our curves, be proud of our breasts (big or small) be proud of how our body moves, and be proud of our femininity and the power that comes from this. Us women *all* have a beautiful, sexy, powerful and sensual Goddess inside of us, but we seem to lose her, whether it be through relationships, having children, or just life's opinions on what's acceptable and what's not. There was a time where I shut out the more sensual and sexy part of myself, due to the abuse and innocence which was taken away from me as a child. The older I grew and the more 'spiritual' my path became, the more I believed it may not be appropriate to embrace and 'show off' to the world, to others, or even to myself this side of me. Societal conditioning was definitely also a big factor in this. I felt somehow wrong or dirty by feeling proud of my body and embracing every inch of it. The more I spoke of this with other women, the more I realized how I wasn't alone in these thoughts. I realized just how deep the conditioning of society makes women grow up believing that to be perceived in a certain light we *must* act a certain way, dress a certain way, walk and talk a certain way. But the truth is we *do* each have a choice to stand up and say no! This is *my* body, *my* life, and as long as I am not hurting anyone I can live in any way *I* choose!

To me, there's nothing more beautiful than a woman who is comfortable in her own skin, unapologetically herself. It's not just freeing and liberating to us, it's also freeing and liberating to all women who cross our path. There will always be someone who disagrees, but that's ok, that's life, what's not ok is when we allow *another* to determine who *we* are going to be. The moment we do this is the moment we conform, lose our power, along with our birthright in the process. We *can* still be a sensual and sexy woman of the Earth who holds much value and respect for herself. Even upon a spiritual path, because fundamental a true spiritual path is a path of truth, a path of embracing all which we are, and a path that lives in full alignment with self.

So find that balance in your own unique beauty, learn to love *Her,* learn to bring the Goddess out and be proud of all she is.

keep her part of you always. it's your right as a woman!

JUST FOR TODAY...

Forgive Yourself

There is always talk of forgiveness for others, but what about forgiveness for self? I've found this to be the most challenging.

When someone has treated us badly, however severe, the wrong is *their* doing and they are the ones which have to live with that. Even if it takes years, overtime I believe we can learn to release the hate, anger, or pain that another has caused our heart and let go. Though this can be challenging and extremely hard at times, depending on the circumstance, I feel it to be sometimes easier than forgiving and letting go of the pain *we* have caused another or the pain *we* cause ourselves. Self-forgiveness can be a much more challenging thing to do as we first have to admit that we were wrong and take self-responsibility which can be one of the hardest things to do, out of fear - fear of looking weak, fear of being vulnerable, fear of looking bad etc. Knowing that we did wrong or made a mistake, especially a big one, leaves a lot of guilt in our thoughts and our energy which can be hard to shift. We can feel that if we don't carry the guilt around month after month or year after year then we can't be sorry for what we did, but the truth is, believing that we have to feel guilt for a long time to truly be sorry for what we did is just the lies our mind tells us. My experiences have shown me that guilt can be like a dark shadow - shielding our heart from the light getting in and also from giving it out.

So you messed up, it's done! Forgive yourself, make the necessary steps to change what you can and move forward or stay stuck. Say you're sorry if you have to, even if you can only say it to your own heart, and try to do better next time.

You, as much as anyone, deserves forgiveness.

JUST FOR TODAY...

Live 'Out' Of The Moment

When people say *'to be truly happy you need to live in the moment'* I believe this to be true in some form, for example - when your life is pretty settled and you don't really have many struggles apart from the struggles which you are creating in your own mind, then living in the moment can be beautiful! But what if the moment you're living in is hell? Many people around the world through no fault of their own haven't got the luxuries that others have and living in the moment for them could be more painful than not. In this case, I believe that to find some happiness we need to take ourselves *out* of the moment and turn our energy and focus to something beautiful in the future. Be it a job, a new relationship, new surroundings, a new venture, or simply a new you! It's called having faith. When we are at our lowest and life and up against the tides, we all need a little faith to keep us moving forward, helping to give us a little smile in our hearts when we feel there's nothing to smile for. Sometimes we need to take ourselves *out* of the moment to make living in the moment that little more comfortable.

So, live in the moment if the moment you are living in is beautiful, otherwise, keep the faith, knowing inside your heart that *your* beautiful moment is just around the corner.

JUST FOR TODAY...

Step Away From The Crowd, Your life Awaits You

I'm a true, Wild, Free-Spirited Woman of the World! I don't allow myself to get too attached to others and I don't like it when others get too attached to me. As one of my favorite quotes states *'if I give them the power to feed me I also give them the power to starve me'* (by Dr. Steve Maraboli). I don't have one specific best friend as I wouldn't want to class one person more special than another. To me, they're all special in their own beautiful unique ways. They all teach me different things and fulfil different needs at different stages of my life, just like I do with them. I believe that we weren't meant to cling to one person, but give as much of ourselves as we can to as many people as we can, sharing and caring with lots of different souls - old, young, those who speak a different language, those from a different social class and those from different religions etc. passing on knowledge and wisdom that we have learnt, and in return taking knowledge and wisdom from others, forever learning and experiencing this precious life we've been given.

Sticking to the old makes no room for spiritual growth. Of course this doesn't mean you must leave everyone behind, it simply means don't ever feel you are obliged to stay around those who aren't willing to grow alongside you. After all, we don't learn by what we already know, we learn by what we don't, by the different, by the uncomfortable and the new. It's the same as courage, strength, truth, self-worth and confidence in ourselves, we can only gain this amazing and powerful inner growth by stepping out of the familiar in life and realising that we're not going to fall apart. Sometimes, to become who we really want to become we need to break away from the past in all its forms so we can truly move forward into a brand new future. We need to learn how to unearth the inner courage so we can break any chains of attachment, whether that attachment be to people or to a certain path we believe we *should* be walking. You are not tied to anyone or anything, and no one holds ownership of you, but you *do* owe it to yourself and the one beautiful short life you've been given to create an amazing human being who is overflowing with love, which then overflows to those you touch.

If only you realised just how powerful you really are, just how much your own light could shine and how all you ever need to become all you wish to be is right inside of you, you'd amaze yourself at the things you can achieve.

So breathe in deeply and find *your* path.

Life is waiting.

JUST FOR TODAY...

Raise Your Standards

- It's ok to want the best
- It's ok to want to be around successful people
- It's ok to want healthy positive energy relationships
- It's ok to watch who you surround yourself with
- It's ok to say no
- It's ok to say yes
- It's ok to aim to be the very best at what you do
- It's ok to expect to be treated in a kind, respectful manner
- It's ok to befriend whoever you want and steer clear of those you don't want
- It's ok to not accept lies

- It's ok to not follow the crowd
- And it's ok to raise your standards in any way you choose!

Doing this does not mean you're putting others down or judging them in anyway, it simply means you see your *own* self-worth, you see the Woman that *you* wish to become and that you're honoring this in the best way you know how. When growing and moving from one state of being to the next; spiritually, emotionally, physically etc. you'll begin to realise relationships surrounding you will also begin to shift and change. Know this is normal, but never allow the uncomfortableness of others to deter your growth. If you want to be the very best you must surround yourself with the very best. I'm not talking materialistic,

I'm talking about the good, motivational, true, inspiring, passionate, non-judgmental doers and positive energy people of the world as *these* are the ones who truly make the difference and will want to celebrate in your victories when you rise.

So don't ever feel bad for raising *your* standards, if some don't like it, maybe it's time they raised theirs.

JUST FOR TODAY...

Meditate

When we pray we speak to the Goddess, but when we meditate we allow the Goddess to speak to us

Meditation isn't religious and there is no right or wrong way to do it. It is simply being still, quieting (not eradicating) your thoughts and coming back to you. When we close our eyes, breathe deeply and literally bring our awareness within, in this silence we create a stillness so that *She* can speak. We start looking into our own hearts and truly feeling *our* truth instead of the outside chatter.

When you first start to meditate you can find your mind jumping all over the place, the Buddhists call this 'the monkey mind'.

Thoughts from yesterday or worries of tomorrow seem to consume our whole being, but over time we can learn to build a control over our thoughts instead of our thoughts having a control over us. Don't think that meditation is about totally cutting out the inner voice, this is not true, we will always have some sort of inner dialog going on, but when we meditate we learn to first accept our feelings, our thoughts, acknowledge them, then we allow them to pass us on by, like clouds in the sky. We build an inner strength and a patience, which helps us to let go of those things we can't control and gain greater focus on what we can.

When I meditate it's like going home and reconnecting with the most sacred overwhelming love and acceptance there is.

It's like opening up my *'internal eye of wisdom and knowledge'* where I come back to my *true* self and know all will be well. There's a place deep within my heart, deep within all of our hearts, where something greater touches our soul. Answers come to us and feelings get released, all assisting us in returning to ourselves, to the truth, and to love.

Even the word meditate has *'me'* at the beginning,

and *'me'* is where all beginnings should start.

JUST FOR TODAY...

Make A Promise To Yourself

When we make a promise to ourselves and stick to it we feel within us a deep sense of achievement, a sense of worth, and a spiritual weight lifts. By following through with something which has been hanging around in our hearts shows us that we *can* do whatever we focus our energy towards. With every promise made and every promise kept, an inner strength grows inside, over time helping us to continue to grow in strength and push us through any fears which have restricted us from moving forward in the past.

Keeping a promise is a beautiful thing to keep with anyone, especially ourselves. The belief in who we are and the trust we have in our own capabilities comes down to our integrity and sticking to our words by 'walking the walk'. This is the greatest truth we can show to the world, as it's not just the words we speak that define us, it's our character, who we are day in and day out and the actions we take which show others our true self.

So have a think about all you wish to achieve, complete, or pursue, and all you wish to become, then make that promise and carry it out. You will be amazed at how empowered you feel when you stick to what you say and finally complete something you never thought you would!

JUST FOR TODAY...

Question

However many of the same things you may read, hear about, or are told, don't be afraid to question it all!

I've never fully understood why many of us humans tend to 'just go along' with the words of the world, after all, it was only one human which first created a thought, a sentence, a way of being, or what's deemed as correct or not, so why can't *you* or *I* be that human being which creates the next first of something? Don't believe every word you read, don't listen to every voice that speaks, and don't go along with others if it doesn't feel right within your own heart. Even *my* words, *these* very words which you are reading now are just my own thoughts and perceptions, my own wisdom and my own beliefs, based on my own life's experiences which may well differ to yours. This is ok. If something which I've written resonates deep within you then I'm happy that we've connected in some way, if it doesn't, question it, find your own answers and never be scared to discover more. I find it a truly beautiful thing when I see another soul who isn't scared to question. I love hearing how other people can perceive things as this is where more learning can be made. I've had many people say to me 'why do you question everything?' like it's a bad thing, and I just reply 'why not?!'

The greatest reply for many things, if I may say so myself!

JUST FOR TODAY...

Look Within Your Heart

There's no greater power than the power within each of us

Every time you look outside of yourself for the answers or for healing, you dis-empower the greatness that is you! We are not separate from the Earth, we *are* the Earth, we are not separate from the Universe, we *are* the Universe. Every single bit of energy, love, peace, healing, knowledge, wisdom, light, and power, is already within each of us. We are each a manifestation of heaven and earth combined, without one there wouldn't be the other. We women are each a God-dess of this planet, and the men are each a God. Once we allow ourselves to more deeply be connected to the divine intelligence which lays within each of our hearts, to the source, to our Mother Earth and Father Sky, we become empowered to make great changes and more fully aligned; becoming an open channel of all knowledge, wisdom, peace, light, and love. Sometimes we remember this on our own, other times we need somebody to help us remember – *'There is no more greatness in another than you don't already posses within you'.* So look inside your heart, awaken *your* light, and you'll discover all the power you ever need to become your greatest self!

JUST FOR TODAY...

Say Yes To life!

How many times have you let something incredible in life pass you by because of overthinking about all that may go wrong if you just say yes?

We convince ourselves *'I'm not good enough, I'll look stupid, it will fail anyway'*…(to name but a few), just to make it easier to say no, but somewhere deep inside we feel an inner knowing, an instant regret, wishing we would just embrace the fear, take that leap into the unknown, and open ourselves to more chances.

I've been guilty of talking myself out of many things in the past, allowing my chattering mind to hold me back, then wishing afterwards I had listened to my heart, that inner guidance, and made a different choice. The truth is, when we do finally make that stand to 'just do it' (whatever *it* is) the great inner strength, courage, and empowerment that can arise within us from this leap is hugely liberating and extremely freeing for our soul! The more we say *yes* to life, the more opportunities seem to be presented to us, opportunities to assist us in our evolutionary growth.

Instead of telling yourself *'I can't'* and listening to the lies within the mind which make you think about all which could go wrong, go into your heart, where that 'voiceless voice' and knowing resides, whispering to you all the things which could go right!

The thing is, fear isn't to be overcome but is to be understood and embraced.

When we feel fear consuming our whole being it's there for us to *step* in to and grow.

So, take *life's liberating leap* into *yes* and remember:

If you truly want your life to change and become someone you've never been, you'll have to do something you've never done!

JUST FOR TODAY...

Stay Humble

However much you achieve in this life and however far you've come, stay humble, knowing that life could take it all away within an instant.

There's nothing wrong with feeling enormously grateful, overwhelmingly happy, and a little proud of yourself for your achievements, but it's also good to keep yourself grounded, remembering where you came from and remembering the struggles.

Offering to lend a hand to those less fortunate is one of the most beautiful acts of kindness you can do once you have got to where you have.

Staying humble keeps us connected to spirit which helps send an energy through our heart in all we do, helping us to actually succeed more in the long run than those who would have been driven by ego.

Staying humble resonates an energy and an attitude which says;

'I am no better than you and you are no better than me, we are just different souls at different stages of our journey'.

So, when you succeed, and your life becomes rich in the many ways it can, grow bigger in your heart, not in your head.

JUST FOR TODAY...

Share Your Scars

When inspiring others or showing empathy and understanding, people don't want to only hear about your triumphs and successes, they want to also see what pain you've had, what you've pulled through and all that you've managed to conquer, as this helps them to connect with you more deeply, giving them hope and helping them to see 'if someone else can come through all of that then so can I'.

Being 'real' means being *all* that you are and showing this to others, warts and all. This allows people to see that you are indeed very human and haven't just got to where you are because of some great life which has got you there. This is sometimes something many of us can assume when we see someone doing well. We think that they must have had it easy or couldn't have been through much.

Sharing your scars is a very humble and vulnerable but very beautiful way of connecting at a deeper level with someone, whether it's a friend, family, on a platform, or even your clients in a business.

Always remember that your scars have added to making you who you are today. Every single one, big or small. Never hide from them or feel ashamed to let others see their depth.

Sharing this way helps the light of truth shine from your heart and out to those around you, giving a beautiful congruent nature which is the best thing to have when wanting to truly connect with anyone and have them connect with you in return.

JUST FOR TODAY...

Believe In The Journey

You may not understand things sometimes, you may not even like how things unfold. The whys and how's of life can all get so confusing, making us question ourselves and everything we do.

The message here is simply to believe;

- *Believe* that there is a reason for your past
- *Believe* that there is a reason for your pain
- *Believe* that there is a reason for past relationships
- *Believe* there is a reason why that door didn't open up for you
- *Believe* that there is a reason for your journey

Most importantly, *believe* in yourself, knowing that regardless of who you are or where you are in life, you *do* have the power to change direction at any given time and choose again.

It may be hard and some of those changes will definitely take time, but as long as you keep a strong belief in who you are, reminding yourself that the Universe has your back, then anything is possible.

All it takes is a little belief.

JUST FOR TODAY…

Fill Yourself Up First

As a mother there have been many moments where I've felt extremely guilty about putting myself first, but the more life passed by, the more I realised that to keep being a better mother, a better friend, a better teacher, or just a better person all round, I *had* to put my wants and my needs first in order to make me feel whole and build on *my* inner love, so then I had more love to give to others.

When we forget about ourselves and live for the world, we don't give our best, and in the long run can do more harm than good. On the other hand, when we fuel our own fire so that it is burning brightly, it helps to keep our energy high and our hearts full with love so then we have more loving energy to give.

People get the best of us when we first give the best to ourselves.

Filling ourselves up can be done in so many ways, whether it be taking up a hobby or a job we've always wanted, making 'me' time, starting a new project, getting on a course or having regular girly holiday's away etc. anything that is just for you.

So, don't forget this.

Do your own thing and find a way to let *your* light shine so you can then take that light and shine it on others.

JUST FOR TODAY…

Write Yourself A Love Letter

Imagine you have to write a letter to someone you deeply love, someone you think is amazing and someone you look up to.

This someone is you!

When you begin to write you may think to yourself 'I can't write that!' or you may think what you're writing may sound 'big headed'. It's not! I'm giving you permission to big yourself up! Write about how proud you are of your strengths (no weaknesses in this letter), write about the beautiful parts of your body and your personality, and write about your talents no matter how small, write it all!

Tricky isn't it?

The thing is, we so rarely talk with love and kindness about ourselves that we forget *how* to! We seem to find it easier when it comes to loving others, but what about loving all who *we* are? Is that not that important too? Where did we learn that it's not ok to love ourselves and be proud of this?

The world gives us an attitude which says 'look at her, who does she think she is?' or 'she thinks she's too good!' When actually it's not you at all, it's others most likely not feeling good enough within themselves, and *your* strength just amplifies this. I only think loving who we are becomes a problem if we're putting others down for who *they* are. If we're not, we should be allowed to be whomever we choose and show the world 'it doesn't matter if others don't love me, *I* love me and I'm happy with the woman I am!'

So write that love letter, even post it to yourself if you wish, then start believing in the beautiful miracle which you are.

It's ok, you are aloud to be kind to yourself too!

JUST FOR TODAY...

She Surrendered

She surrendered to the pain, the confusion, the fears, and the doubt.

She surrendered to not knowing all of the answers, to the unknown, and to all she couldn't control.

She surrendered to not having it all, to the struggle, to the fight, and to the worry of how she believed things 'should' be.

She surrendered to her flaws, her 'not getting it quite right' and her imperfectly perfect self, remembering how every single physical and emotional scar shows that SHE is a survivor.

She surrendered to how others saw her, what others may or may not have thought, realising it's more important how SHE sees herself.

She surrendered to the inner exhaustion, the body crying out for rest, and the mind shouting out for peace.

She surrendered to finally listening to the quiet whispers within, the tears longing to fall, the pain longing to be seen, and the sadness longing to be loved.

She surrendered...More deeply than ever before, and without saying a word, SHE allowed her heart to finally be free

JUST FOR TODAY...

Make Friends With Negativity

When we're being negative, i.e. angry, bitter, resentful, jealous, judgmental, low, insecure or hurt, these are feelings that have crept up inside us over time that need to be released, but if they aren't, these negative feelings get stronger. They build up and up inside, trying to tell us 'I want out, my job is done, it's now up to you to release me', but too often than not we won't let them go, not in the right ways anyway. How we release them in the right way is;

- Firstly - we need to come to an *awareness* that they are there.

- Secondly - we need to understand *why* they are there.
- Thirdly - we need to *face* them and take self-responsibility to change them before we can move forward.

Only when we have done these three things we can truly start to let them go. When we do, these feelings rise to the surface and come out with talking, crying, or both, and it feels like a weight slowly lifting. In time, we start to feel the great peace that comes from this, maybe not in the beginning as feelings usually hurt before they can get better, but when they do lift, our energy starts to shift and change, we start to feel more positive, lighter, stronger, focused, get more of an understanding of who we are, we're less confused, and we become even more aware of ourselves then we ever have been, but you see, none of this could be possible without experiencing those negative feelings in the first place. It's only through our sufferings we can learn to appreciate and grow.

Negativity is like an emotional poison which starts off as something very small, but through our own minds, set ways of thinking, and resistance to change, it begins to grow into something much bigger and powerful, infecting our whole system. It's only when we hold on to these feelings longer then we need that we endure constant suffering and pass that suffering on to others. I now look at negativity as a friend who is trying to tell me 'something isn't right' 'something needs to change' or 'it's time to let go now'.

JUST FOR TODAY…

Be Grateful

Gratitude is a beautiful thing, it opens up your heart and lets more in.

Those that are truly grateful for things in their life begin to create an energy of pure love and appreciation that flows through their heart and soul and out to all the beautiful things in their life, creating more beautiful things to be grateful for; in the present, and in the future. This may not always happen in the way we thought, but continuing to feel true gratitude *will* begin to manifest more and more beauty in the most incredible ways!

Over the years I've learnt not to hold on to what's gone (or who's gone) but look forward to what *will* be and appreciate all I *do* have instead of all I don't. I choose not to waste my precious thoughts and energy on situations or people from my past that may not have worked out, I see no reason in doing so. Things happen, people leave, mistakes are made, but that's life. In every given moment we each have a choice to let go and move forward, or hold on and stay stuck. It really is that simple. Make a conscious choice to keep peace in your heart so you can still give kindness to all, especially those who do you wrong. Prioritize who and what's important, focus on your own life instead of another's, and teach yourself to be ok when things don't always work out how you thought. If you find yourself comparing your life to someone else, compare it to what you *do* have and what others who may be less fortunate don't have. Once you learn to truly appreciate more in your own life and the beauty that *you* have been blessed with, there really will be no room for ungratefulness.

So always stay true and appreciative in your heart by showing and more importantly *feeling* true gratitude, and you'll find that the Universe will continue to send more for you to be grateful for!

JUST FOR TODAY...

Break Free

Growing into someone new and letting go of the old can be a very uncomfortable process cant it? But, this is what makes it right! I call these shifts *'the labor pains of life'*.

There are two choices when it comes to change:

We stay where we are, which may be comfortable but not necessarily making us happy,

or

we break free from the prison we have restricted ourselves to and move forward into the unknown, allowing the uncomfortableness of this to flow through us for a while whilst this shift takes place. We can so badly want to move forward, to grow; spiritually, mentally, and emotionally, to achieve dreams we've put off, or to meet new people and take that leap, that sometimes our want can be so powerful, consuming our very being, but we resist and put up a fight, not wanting to step out of the comfort of our womb that we have created, yet knowing deep in our heart that if we don't take that leap we may wither away and stay stuck, but *this* is the moment where we must loosen our grip on the past so we have *both* hands free to grasp our future. You can't become who you want to be and still be who you used to be at the same time, that would be like trying to be a caterpillar and butterfly all at once! Many of us feel life's labor pains and pull back, thinking it means something's wrong, which usually is never the case. The most successful people all had to go through these changes, and the only thing that makes a successful person different to an unsuccessful one is how much they we're willing to lose, to let go of all they *were* so they could become all they *wanted.*

When the fear of staying stuck and not achieving becomes more overwhelming than the fear of facing the labor pains of change, *this* is when you will start to break free and become the woman you were born to be!

JUST FOR TODAY...

Don't Be So Hard On Yourself

Sometimes we just have to give up the fight, let go of who's right and who's wrong, learn to forgive ourselves, kiss the guilt goodbye, stop thinking of the what if's, and just surrender to where the road may take us, because at times this is the only way to heal and let go of who we were so we can become who we are meant to be.

Start by reminding yourself you're doing the best you can in the best way you know how. It's ok to not know all the answers, it doesn't make you bad, it makes you human. Don't be so hard on yourself. Always stay true to your inner voice, and never allow another to sway you from your path. Next time you criticize yourself for getting something wrong, try loving yourself a little more for getting something right.

Remember; Just because we grow up doesn't mean we achieve perfection, so hold your inner child tightly and tell them *'don't worry, you'll be fine, I love you'.*

JUST FOR TODAY...

Walk Away

Are you feeling like you need to walk away from something or someone?

When we walk away from a relationship, a friendship or any situation for that matter, we can sometimes feel that we've failed, or worst still, others can try to make us feel like we have. Well, let me tell you, you haven't! Don't feel bad about choosing to let go of anything or anyone that's in some way damaging for your heart and soul. It's easy for someone to judge or say 'never give up', but to truly know the *whys,* they would have had to be in your exact position and shouldn't really judge at all. Letting go can be an excruciating heart break; mourning the death of what once was, especially if it's a friendship or relationship of some sort that has lasted many years. When we go through this letting go, we finally accept that another's emptiness and pain requires a lot more than we have to give, and that we are no longer prepared to hand over our whole life and soul to someone who doesn't care about their own.

You haven't been given your beautiful life to only be that light for someone else.

The truth is, real failure doesn't come from giving up on others, it only truly comes from giving up on yourself.

JUST FOR TODAY

Keep Quiet

When faced with criticism, harsh words, or opinions we don't agree with, it can be hard to keep our mouths shut, but this is what is needed at times. We are always going to come up against adversity, those who disagree or those who will never see past the end of their nose, how we deal with them is to keep quiet! Don't feel you're losing or allowing them to control you, this isn't the case. It takes more power and control to realise when your words will fall on deaf ears rather than to go into battle with those set on fighting, if you do, you're actually just giving them what they want!

Your opinions are precious and deserve recognition, but with the right people who will welcome them warmly in loving and open discussions, just as it should be; without drama, without fight, without fuss!

Being this way does not stop us from having an opinion or a voice, it's just a little reminder to make sure your energy won't be wasted on the *wrong* people. I've found it's actually those who are unsure about themselves which have the most persistant voice. A confident and wise person doesn't feel the *need* to defend, attack, or convince others that they are wise or why they think or feel the way they do, they recognise and understand that everyone is different, and that this is ok. They respect the voice of another, even if it differs to their own, and they walk around with an inner smile, a comfortableness within themselves that says *'I am me and you are you, I accept this'.*

So remember the next time someone tries to push your buttons just to get a reaction, just smile, a smile of acceptance, not agreement, and keep *your* inner and outer voice peaceful and quiet.

JUST FOR TODAY...

Stay True

Remind yourself that your journey is your own; unique and individual. It doesn't matter if people understand it or agree with it as it's not their life to make sense of, it's yours. No other person will ever truly understand what your life is about until they have lived it. Your job is simply just to breathe, just to love, just to learn, and just to be you in the truest form that you can be. If you can master this, I promise, the rest will take care of itself.

A little positive affirmation for you;
All I can be is the best I can be,
It may never be good enough for some,

But I'll continue to stay true and to always be me, as staying true means I've already won.

JUST FOR TODAY...

Feel Instead Of Thinking

When caused with a dilemma in our lives, however big or small, to make a decision is it best to *think* with our heads or *feel* with our hearts?

Personally, I've learnt over many years to do what feels right within my heart, that inner guidance and voiceless voice we all have deep inside. Even if there's been hurt and struggle whilst moving forwards, feeling what's in my heart seems to give me an inner glow and a *knowing* of where I'm walking is on the right path. You see, our heart is connected to our soul, and our soul always knows what's best.

A great phrase I like is; *'Constant analysis can cause paralysis'*

For me this means that the more we think about the 'right' thing to do the more this actually stops us from moving forward with our heart and our true feelings.

When we think too much, I feel it's more about our ego and what's right for others rather than what's right for us.

I truly believe we have to just learn go where our heart takes us, even if things don't turn out exactly how we thought, keeping the trust and faith that as long as we follow our inner divine guidance, everything will be beautiful.

JUST FOR TODAY...

Be Open To Receive

Everyone needs a little help at times, a little assistance, an outstretched hand, a word of encouragement or an ear willing to listen. No one gets where they are fully on their own, even though the initial steps do come from inside of us, we all need that extra lift once in a while. Never be too proud to ask for help, take advice and be open to receive from others. At times in the past I myself have been much too proud to ask for help, thinking that it was a weakness, worrying that showing my struggles or my vulnerability would put me in a powerless position and under attack, but the truth is, when you ask and receive help from the *right* people they realise your struggles and openly admit the struggles they too have experienced. This greatly helps you to realise that you're not alone in how you feel and there *is* light at the end of the tunnel! Asking for help and being open to receive actually leaves you enormously empowered! We have to be aware of *who* we are sharing ourselves with as not everyone's intentions are to help, but sharing your scars, your fears or your tears with the *right* people and letting someone else in once in a while, will not just help another in knowing that they aren't alone, it will heal a little part of your own heart also.

JUST FOR TODAY...

Be The One In Ten

It takes heaps of strength and courage to stand alone, to be different than the rest, to risk losing friends or family because of your choice to stay true to yourself and not 'follow the crowd'. When this happens you may find others saying 'she's changed' or 'she thinks she's too good', when in reality by standing alone you've just stopped living a life to constantly please others, you've stopped living in such a way that makes others feel comfortable and you've started focusing on your own journey instead.

To stand alone and to be that one in ten doesn't mean you're lonely and it doesn't mean you're doing something wrong, you're actually doing something right. We weren't put on this beautiful earth to be the same as the rest. You only have to look at the great hearts, the peace makers, the writers, and the creative people of the world to realise this truth. *These* were the ones that at times were considered strange, weird or eccentric, as they were hugely different than the rest and quite reclusive, but it's these incredible hearts who chose not to listen to the world that made the biggest difference. It was the ones singled out by society that ended up being the most inspirational.

The ones who can't walk alone or choose not to are usually those who are too scared to have a voice of their own, who have a huge need to 'fit in' with the rest (even if it means fitting in with the wrong ones) and who are too scared to walk their own path in case no one walks with them, but what happens in the long run is they've been so busy trying to 'fit in' with others that they've forgotten how to make an authentic life of their own, then before they know it life has passed them by and the journey hasn't been their journey at all.

Albert Einstein said:

"The woman who follows the crowd will usually go no further than the crowd. But the woman who walks alone is likely to find herself in places no one has ever been before".

So make that stand *your* stand. You never know who you may inspire.

JUST FOR TODAY…

Smile

People should smile more!

Whether you're the smiler (the one who starts the smile) or the smile-ee (the one who smiles back!) either way is good. A smile, especially one done from the heart, literally lights up you face, lights up your eyes and helps to light up a room! It helps others to feel acknowledged and also shows kindness. Think about how lovely it is when *you* receive a smile, especially from someone who doesn't even know you! It's a beautiful feeling isn't it? We can pull back a smile in fear of the 'what ifs', *'what if they don't smile back?'* or *'what if they think I'm a little mad?!'*

It doesn't matter if they don't smile back, that's not what you're doing it for, you're doing it for them, to show another a little kindness, to perhaps brighten up another's day even if just a little. They may not smile back because you may have caught them off guard, they may think you're smiling at someone else, or they may have just forgot their glasses!

Whatever the reason may be, *you* will feel good for it.

So go out and smile that big beautiful smile of yours! The world needs more people who take time to smile, and it may be the only bit of kindness someone's had all day.

JUST FOR TODAY...

Love Your Temple

The most amazing, precious, and sacred thing you will ever fully own is your body. Without it you would not be able to do all the everyday little things that we all so often take for granted. It is 'Gods vehicle' which has been lent to you to journey in this life with, and if not looked after properly or given an MOT once in a while, it will simply conk out and start shutting down. First the internal work will misbehave which will then start showing externally, disabling you from moving through life with ease through any path you wish to venture on.

It's such an important thing to watch all that our body intakes, but the *most* important thing is our internal energy, what's going on with our thoughts, how much unwanted 'stuff' we're holding onto and how we're keeping our spirit balanced.

Listen to your body. If you need sleep, then sleep, if you need to eat healthy then eat healthy, if you need to give up certain habits then give them up, if you need to diet then diet, if you need to release and let go then do it! We all know what our body is trying to tell us, we can *feel* it, but more often than not we ignore it and make excuses, then we wonder why we've fallen apart.

Look at your body as a safe haven to retreat to, the one place that will never let you down, a place to feel at home in where you will forever be loved and supported, but to keep this beautiful exchange going you need to love and support it back.

It truly is the greatest temple on earth, so look after it.

JUST FOR TODAY...

Get Out Of Your Own Way

No one is more in control of your life than you and don't tell yourself otherwise for a second, as the more we convince ourselves of something the more we believe it to be true.

We all want to be seen, to be heard, to be understood, and to be accepted and loved. We all have dreams and hopes of how we would like to see our life and our future, but we build up walls around ourselves, we build up unreasonable fears and we make excuses as to why we aren't doing something that we want, but in truth, the only person hindering our growth, is us.

We are our own worst enemies and our worst critics, but we can also be our greatest savior. People can lend you a hand, an encouraging word or show you a door, but like it or not, it's *you* that has to walk through it and make that conscious effort to take those first steps into change.

When are you going to realise your full potential? Even the greatest had to start at the bottom, and the only thing that separates them from you is that they made a choice to move forward into their fear rather than allow their mind to keep them stuck.

So now's the time to get out of your own way and move forward once and for all.

JUST FOR TODAY...

Set Your Boundaries

We can't choose how others treat us but we *can* choose what we do about it through the boundaries we put in place. We can either allow them to carry on crossing those lines or let them know when something is just not acceptable. Some will respect this, others won't, and it's the ones that won't that you will need to let go of.

It is us which teach people how to treat us. How much we are prepared to put up with comes down to how much self-worth and self-respect we have.

When you come across certain people who treat you a certain way or think it's 'ok' to cross certain boundaries, this comes down to how much respect they have for themselves and others, and also what others have allowed them to get away with in the past. I've met a few people like this throughout my own life who almost can't believe when I stand up for myself or show my boundaries and let them know exactly what I won't put up with. I've even had someone say to me before 'so and so doesn't mind' or 'I don't mind when so and so does this to me'. They seem to think or believe that just because someone else has allowed something before that everyone is going to allow it. These kind of people don't seem to realise that this is all down to just how much respect another has for themselves. Some less than others.

The message here is to know your worth and know you are well within your right to ask for respect from those who cross the line. The ones that understand and respect your boundaries will respect your requests, it's only the ones which either don't have much respect for themselves or have been allowed to cross many boundaries before, are the ones which will try to make you feel wrong, and most likely walk away, usually because they can't get away with anything they want, but do not chase them as they are being removed from your life for a purpose.

So, respect others boundaries and always stand strong in yours.

JUST FOR TODAY...

Listen With Your Heart

Are you *really* listening?

Many of us think we are, but usually we are listening to respond, not listening to understand.

When someone comes to us to speak about their pains or their joys, all they truly want from another is to be understood, to be heard and to be accepted without judgment. We can only listen this way if we close our ears; the door way to our ego, and open up our *hearts hearing* instead.

When we fully and deeply *hear* exactly what someone is trying to say, an energy absorbs and surrounds our heart, helping us to really *feel* their words and connecting us on a deeper level, and it's only when people feel truly heard is when they start to heal.

So open up your heart instead of your ears, you'll be surprised at how much you can get to know someone when you learn to look past the words and *feel* the soul.

JUST FOR TODAY...

Be Passionately Peaceful

Being peaceful isn't just about being still, being quiet, or being calm, you can be a very passionate and high energy person and still be filled with much peace. Being at peace is all about *who* you are and how you *feel* about yourself and your life. This all comes down to how content you are with your journey.

Learning to align our surroundings to what feels right *within* brings an enormous amount of peace. To do this we must find our passion, the thing that makes us feel alive and sets our heart and soul on fire. We must learn to follow this as it will lead us to our purpose. People talk of inner peace but rarely talk of *how* to find it, but through my own experiences I have found that this beautiful inner peace comes when we are living and breathing a life which is authentic and fulfilling. I call this *passionately peaceful.*

From personal experience I truly believe that by finding our greatest passion and taking the necessary steps to fulfilling this internal fire that burns within our heart, we then find the peace we've been searching for.

JUST FOR TODAY...

You Are Enough

To be someone special, you don't have to be anyone or anything else but you!

You don't have to be famous, you don't have to be known by thousands, you don't have to be in a high paying job or have a particular 'status', you don't need the best clothes or the biggest house and you don't have to have hundreds of friends.

Being 'enough' is just trying to be a better person than you were yesterday, it's being kind, it's learning from your mistakes, it's living in peace with others, it's giving love to those next to you, it's growing stronger from life's struggles, it's getting back up after you have fallen, and it's putting your heart in all you do.

Being 'enough' has nothing to do with *what* you do, it's *who* you are, embracing yourself fully, inside and out, your strengths and your weakness's, and not needing anything or anyone else to fill you up.

We only feel not good enough when we know there is more to us inside and we aren't living with integrity.

So take each day as it comes, do the best you can with where you are, and remind yourself; you are beautiful, you are special, and you are enough…Just as you are.

JUST FOR TODAY…

Cut Your Cords

From early childhood through to adult years we each unconsciously attach to others or have others attach to us *invisible energy cords.* These are a little like umbilical cords, but instead of feeding us nutrition and love, they usually feed us lower energy, hurt, pain and literally 'attach' our energy field to one another, hooking us into different emotional patterns and draining each other's energy. Either way is not good. Have you ever felt, be it with a family member, friend, or past relationship, that you just can't quite shake their energy, you feel overly dependent on them or you still feel like they have some sort of hold over you even though they aren't around? This is all because of the invisible but very real energy cords that are still attached from them to us or from us to them. What's happening is that the energy from either side flows down these 'umbilical cords' and manifests into us and all that we are which then comes out in our aura and even our thought patterns.

Don't fear that cutting cords with those you still love will stop that love, it won't, all it will do is help to release any 'stuck' energy which has been given to you from them or given to them from you, helping to clear and empower your energy force and allow you to get back to your true self, whoever that may be, without the influence of another's energy.

How you can start to cut these ties and release the burdens they bring is to first be aware as to who *your* cords are connected to and who you feel has connected *theirs* to you, then feel deeply you're your heart, asking the Divine source to lovingly sever these ties so that you may start healing.

This process can take time, but once you begin unravelling these cords and cutting where needed, you will start to feel a lightness in yourself, emotionally, physically and mentally, feeling like you can breathe deeply once again and return to *your* truth.

JUST FOR TODAY...

Keep Focused On Your Dreams

Life has a very good and very sneaky way of swaying us off our path, if we allow it. We can be soaring along beautifully without a care in the world, then a great wind comes which forces us to change direction for a while. Sometimes this can be for a good reason, other times it's to test us, to see just how strong and focused we are on achieving all we want and to see how determined we are to bring the sails back in to carry on down the path we were heading. I'm encouraging you to keep your head forward, do not allow those around you, those from the past, or the 'wolves in sheep's coats' to turn your head in any way. Remember who you are and where you're heading. We can also get disheartened by our journey and the dreams we are hoping to create. We ask ourselves at times 'will it work? Am I good enough? What about this or that?' so many questions and thoughts can run through our head hindering us from carrying on. When this happens (because it will) remind yourself *why* you are doing what you are doing and all the great things which will come into your life and your heart from sticking to your true path.

So stay focused at all times and never allow anyone or anything to stop you from achieving your dreams.

They are yours…protect them.

JUST FOR TODAY…

Claim Back Your Power

There's many strong, high energy, opinionated, and very powerful people in this world, which isn't always a bad thing, but sometimes, to those that may not feel as strong, these extremely high energy people can make you feel (unintentionally or not) like you have to 'go along' with them and their needs. Many of them don't mean to come across like this, they are just very sure of who they are and what they want, which in all honesty, I admire this, but if our energy isn't feeling quite as high as theirs or we're going through a bit of a rough patch, we will find we tend to agree with them when we don't actually want to agree, we say yes when we want to say no, we find ourselves apologizing for nothing and overly justifying our reasons when we do speak up. It's time to claim back *your* power! Doing this does not need to be done in an aggressive, confrontational, or angry way, it's simply about remembering who *you* are, what *your* needs are, without feeling guilty or that you have to justify, and learning to say no once in a while, or yes if you really want to.

Remind yourself that people only really have a hold over you if you think it or allow it, so allow it not, and be the strong woman that you are!

JUST FOR TODAY...

Sit In Silence

We all need quiet time to ourselves once in a while. I'm talking about *real* quiet time; no TV, no books, no talking to friends or family, no Internet, no music, just us. Very few take this precious time out, but it's extremely essential for our spirit, as it's in this time, this alone silent space, that our spirit talks and the real us emerges. If you feel yourself searching for an answer you must take time out from the world for however long you feel is needed and be willing to hear the truth within your heart. The whys, the how's, the what ifs, the fears, the guilt etc. all need to be understood before we can start to accept and let go, only then will the answers come, but we must be willing to just *be* in our own silence before we can hear *our* inner voice, *our* inner truth, *our* inner wisdom, and make those necessary changes.

Far too often we allow the noise of the outer world and the people around us to drown out this voice. We do this consciously and sub-consciously for many different reasons; maybe we don't feel ready to hear or face the truth, maybe we know our truth but feel scared at speaking up for fear of what others may say, maybe we don't like criticism, maybe we have a want to always please others with what they want, or maybe we just get so wrapped up in our external world that we forget to take time to listen to our own hearts, thus making ourselves feel more confused, more uneasy, more detached and more lost, all the time not realising that we are the ones that hold the key to the door where the veil lifts and all our answers will unfold.

All it takes is a little silence *without* so we can then hear the little voice *within.*

JUST FOR TODAY...

Don't Worry

Sometimes we can worry so much about how other people are being and put an enormous amount of our time, focus, and energy, on what choices *their* making, what wrong *their* doing, who *they* are or how *their* living in *their* lives that we forget ourselves. This does absolutely nothing apart from waste our time and energy, ruin our day and make us feel uptight and sometimes a little insecure.

We feel worrying will 'prepare' us in some way, but it won't! More importantly it will drain our beautiful energy and keep us stuck, unhappy, and in fear, usually in fear of things that may never happen.

So in these moments, stop, breathe and repeat this powerful prayer:

God, grant me the serenity
To accept the things I cannot change,
Courage to change the things I can,
and the wisdom to know the difference.
(By Reinhold Niebuhr)

Try putting all your energy and all those thoughts into *your* life, what wrongs *you're* doing, the choices *you're* making and who *you* are. Once you start to re-direct your focus and concentrate your energies into your own being, you will accomplish so much more, whilst also being happier and more contented as a whole.

JUST FOR TODAY...

Choose What You Can, Let Go Of The Rest

- You can choose who you'd like as a friend, but you can't choose who'd like you as theirs.
- You can choose the words you speak, but you can't choose how they may effect another.
- You can choose the situations you put yourself in, but you can't choose how those situations will unfold.
- You can choose not to speak ill of another, but you can't choose whether another speaks ill of you.
- You can choose the actions you take, but you can't choose the

consequences of taking those actions.
- You can choose to forgive others, but you can't choose if others forgive you.
- You can choose how you see yourself, but you can't choose how others see you.
- You can choose not to pass judgment on another, but you can't choose whether or not another passes judgment on you.
- You can choose to be a positive person, but you can't choose if others are positive back.

In life, every single one of us has a choice in many things, but those many choices are only choices made within *our* hearts, *our* actions, *our* words, and the paths *we* take, but this is where our choices end. Once you can truly accept this and grasp hold of this truth, life becomes a much simpler place to live. You finally realise that the only person you are truly responsible for is yourself.

If you're a parent, to a degree you are responsible for your children, until they reach an age where they're old enough to make their own choices, however big or small, then they start to become their own responsibility.

Many people don't like the thought of this as they can feel it creates a *'lack of control'*. I personally find it freeing and liberating to know that I'm only responsible for myself. Therefore, I never have to take on what others say, do, or how they act, as personal.

Just take a nice deep breath, forgive the past, let it go, stop blaming others, and just focus on choosing to become the best person you can possibly be.

That's all that life asks of you.

JUST FOR TODAY...

Free Yourself From Those Heavy People

Many of us feel the need to keep heavy (negative) people in our lives. If you are one of them, ask yourself this very simple but to the point question;

Why?

We aren't obliged to keep anyone in our life who doesn't better us or add to our light. Just because you're a good influence for *them* does not mean that they are a good influence for *you,* and if they're not, ask yourself why do you still have them around? Personally I want to enjoy people, not moan about them. We all have the right to spend time with nice people who are positive, passionate, optimistic and like-hearted. Relationships should help you, not hurt you. Surround yourself with people who reflect the person you want to be. Choose friends who you are proud to know, people you admire, people who love and respect *you* in return, and people who make your day a little brighter simply by being in it. Life is too short to be with people who suck the positive energy and happiness out of you. Make sure you know who your friends are as it's better to have an enemy who is open about not liking you rather than a false friend who hugs you but makes you question their loyalty.

You'll realise that when you free yourself from heavy people, you truly free yourself to be you , and being you is the most beautiful way to live.

JUST FOR TODAY...

Do It Your Way

Stop saying yes to others when you really want to say no, and stop saying no to others when deep down you wish you had said yes!

When you're being, acting, and talking in any way, take note of the 'whys' behind it all. Are you truly living for you or for someone else? It could be for your partner, a work colleague, a friend, your family or your children. Do you feel you've been people pleasing just to get along? Have you been following the 'rules' of another's way? If so, stop! You were not put on this earth to be the same as somebody else, after all, it is the difference which makes the difference. What are you afraid of happening if you just be yourself? If you give all the love, kindness, and weirdness that's inside of you to give? If you take a chance on a friendship or relationship? If you do that thing you've always wanted to do? Or if you say the things you've always wanted to say? The truth is, when we commit to truly being ourselves in every way and don't allow others opinions to effect this, it helps our integrity grow which then builds our inner confidence and self-worth.

We waste much more energy by acting in ways that we think we should, rather than just being ourselves, not realising that someone could love the person we are hiding!

Perhaps you're allowing others to control you, believing that if you stand true to yourself and your own way of doing things that you'll be rejected, pushed out, or criticised. If we're not careful, we can get caught up in the crowd and lose who *we* are just to fit in.

So remind yourself of who you truly are, and what your own needs are so you can make that stand, even if it's just a little one. Do it your way, because your way is beautiful too!

JUST FOR TODAY...

Stay Beautiful In Your Heart

People won't always act or respond how *we* do but this isn't what matters. All that matters is how *you* are. Everyone gets what they give out, good and bad, even if it's not from who they expect, it *will* come back in some form or another. This is why it's so important to do our best to find inner happiness, inner peace, and inner love etc. as once you've found this it really is so much easier to give out kindness to another. In my many years of life, I don't just believe, I *know* from all the experiences I've had and seen, that life has a law, the law of karma, there has to be a balance for the bad and the good. When someone is unkind, talks ill of you, lies to you, blames you, tears you down, tries to make you into someone you're not, judges you, puts their poison on you or just finds it impossible to show kindness, all they are truly doing is shining a bright light on their own ugliness, their own unhappiness and their own insecurities, and in the end it's them that has to live with that. This sometimes is their karma; a life full of anger, pain, jealousy, insecurities or unhappiness, which has been created by themselves. There isn't any worse pain then the pain we create within our own hearts and minds, and the more we focus on a certain energy, good or bad, that is the energy we create more of, this is why it is so much more rewarding for ourselves and others around us when we learn to keep our own hearts beautiful and at peace, continuing to shine our lights brightly regardless of how another is.

There's a great Native American quote I like which is;

'There's two wolves inside you fighting, one full of greed, anger, jealousy and hate, the other full of compassion, peace, kindness and love. The wolf which wins is the one you feed'.

So trust that everything happens for a reason, don't take revenge on those who do you wrong, and always stay as beautiful as you can in your own heart, trusting that life will take care of the rest.

JUST FOR TODAY...

Give Peace

For today, right now, as you're reading these words, I would like to wish you peace, straight from my heart. If you would then go on to wish the next person peace and that person wishes the next and so on and so on, then maybe one day we will all have peace.

Each and every one of us can make a positive difference by touching the lives of those around us, by doing this we can cause a ripple effect that spreads out to the whole world! Don't be put off with how big this world is, don't let that fool you into thinking how can *you* possibly make a difference. We can't help everyone, but everyone *can* help someone, whether it be a helping hand, a friendly smile, a listening ear or an encouraging word, however you feel you can spread a little more peace and love, just do it, your kindness might be the only kindness that someone's had.

I truly believe that if we all make a choice to be as beautiful and as loving as we can be to the one standing beside us, then eventually, this world *will* know peace.

JUST FOR TODAY...

Trust Your Heart

Deeply get in touch with your soul, your femininity, and trust what your inner guidance tells you. How many times are you going to beat yourself up for not doing what you knew in your heart you should have done? We have all been born with this beautiful gift called intuition, a feeling and knowing of what's right for us and what's wrong, but we allow ourselves to become so confused, mistrusting ourselves and listening too much to the outer world instead of our inner one. This is all due to a lack of inner connection and over *thinking* with our heads instead of *feeling* with our hearts. Your intuition is that little voice, that feeling deep within that just won't go away. Listen to what it's telling you. If you feel a need to take a little time out to re-connect, do it! This is your heart trying to help lead you to the right path, and instead of giving you what you may think you want, it gives you what you *need*. Even though there may be times you can't see the rest of the road or where it may lead you, that's ok. As long as you keep the faith and listen to your heart, even if it feels a little uncomfortable at first, you will always be guided towards the very best direction for your soul and begin to feel content once again.

That's the funny thing with needs, once they're met, you don't need them anymore!

JUST FOR TODAY...

Know Your Darkness, It's The Only Way Into Your Light

The hardest thing in life isn't giving time to your light, it's giving time to your darkness. It's getting to know every fault, every mistake, every flaw, and every pain, yet greeting them all, being strong and courageous enough to allow them to come to the surface so you can face them head on, understand them, then let them go.

I find the people who have faced their darkness, confronted it, and grown from it, to be the strongest, caring, and most genuine and self-aware people of all. These are the ones who inspire me. They have done the best thing, not only for themselves, but for others, because if we haven't took time to heal *within,* how can we heal *without?* If there has been no self-awareness, no work on your spirit, no keeping grounded, and no working from deep within your heart, whatever your venture in life will be it *will* crumble and fall. It could be months or even years, but it will fall. You need to be sure that you have spiritually and emotionally built a strong foundation before you can build the life you want around you securely.

So have a *feel.* Have you looked inside and faced yourself? Are you truly working from your heart (spirit) or from your head (ego)? Do you crave the praise from others or the praise you are able to give yourself? Why are you doing what you do? Who are you *really* doing it for? What are the long term benefits you're hoping for? Are you doing it to gain or to give, or a little of both? When looking back on your life, what will mean the most to you?

These are just a few very simple questions that you could ask yourself and try to answer honestly. If you find you can't quite answer yet, maybe it's time to just stop, breathe, and face the darkness that you've been trying to hide, as it's only once this darkness has been addressed that the light can then begin to shine through and your heart and be healed.

JUST FOR TODAY...

Thou Shalt Not Judge

Sometimes people just need an ear to listen and a heart to understand, without judgment. Be careful with the energy you're giving out to someone who's in need of a friend. It's not as important as to *what* you say, but more important is your *intention* behind your words and how you feel which will be what comes across to the one who needs to be listened to.

We Women are natural born feelers. We *feel* when someone's truly listening with compassion, empathy, and understanding, and we equally feel when someone's feeling judgmental towards us, regardless of the words they may use.

I've been in this position a few times, like we all have, where I felt judged, but

I've come to understand that the people who judge us are actually the ones with the biggest insecurities, jealousy's, envies, and unhappiness's in their lives, so send them love because their hearts need it the most.

So the next time you're feeling judged, just know that how another judges you is more to do with them then you. If on the other hand you are the one that goes to judge another, look inside and see what's going on.

Breathe in love, breathe out love. Always.

JUST FOR TODAY...

Be Real

Be real.

- Not just in what you say, but how you act.
- Not just in what you hear, but how you listen.
- Not just in front of others, but when no one's looking.
- Not just to someone's face, but behind their back.
- Not just to impress, but because it's right.
- Not just in your talk, but in your walk.
- Not to fit in, but to stand out.

Light comes from truth, love comes from truth, all greatness comes from truth. Truth is easy, truth lifts you up, gives you an inner glow, an inner happiness, connects you to your higher self and to all things beautiful, truth gives you self-worth, self-respect and self-love, truth gives you a deep feeling of being fully at peace with who you are, being able to sit back at the end of each day with a smile on your face and know that 'you did good', truth brings the right people to you and allows the wrong ones to slip away, without you even having to do much. It takes less energy to be truthful and just be yourself. It's those that live in fear, manipulation, control, 'people pleasing', and hiding behind lies which are the people believe truth is hard, but lies are the thing which keeps us spiritually and emotionally weak, they keep us powerless, they diminish our bright light, they destroy us, they draw us to the wrong people and make the right ones slip away, they make us resentful, jealous, bitter and angry, they create anxiety and negativity and all things dark.

The fact is, lies are weak, but truth is powerful. It *yearns* to be seen and it will come out eventually. We can lie to our family, we can lie to our friends, and we can lie to the whole world if we wish, but we can never lie to our own heart.

When we are living in truth, we *know* it, we *feel* it, and we are more at peace within ourselves and others.

JUST FOR TODAY....

Know You're Not Lost

Just take a moment to think of what the word 'lost' means?

When we feel 'lost' it means/feels we don't belong, don't fit in, and don't know where to turn. After feeling into this for a while I then realised that an anagram for 'lost' is 'slot'. The word 'slot' means- *to fit in, to groove, to be assigned to a place or position.* Therefore, think of it like this;

You're not really 'lost', but instead fit perfectly into the right place at the right time, not knowing that life and all that's in it is unfolding all around you, just as it should. Just like a key needs to fit in exactly the right 'slot' for it to turn and open the door up for you, when you're 'lost', Mother Gaia is actually helping you to fit into life's 'slot', so your next path will reveal itself and lead you to the next chapter.

So just remember the next time you feel 'lost', you're not lost at all. The Universe is placing you exactly where you need to be, even if at times you can't see it.

JUST FOR TODAY...

Shine Your Healing Light

I believe that each of us is put on this earth to help others (in the many different ways we can) by giving love, peace, healing, teaching how to connect with their higher selves and the spirit world, and most importantly to show by shining our own great powerful light that it's ok for them to shine theirs without fear of what others will say, or without worry of others being intimidated. We can sometimes worry about being our wonderful selves as we don't want others to feel less of a person around us, or fear we may look 'big headed', but in truth, to truly be who you are, to be confident and happy, to love yourself more and to shine your own unique light is actually what God wants from all of us, and the only ones that may not like your light are the ones still in the dark. Don't allow this to affect you. Continue to shine as brightly as you can because one day you may help another shine with you, bringing out their light within and helping them to see its ok to be all that they are too. As one of my favorite authors says;

"As we let our own light shine, we unconsciously give other people permission to do the same,

As we are liberated from our fear, our presence automatically liberates others"

(Quote taken from 'Our Deepest Fear'-By Marianne Williamson)

So always remember you *are* powerful and free to shine!

JUST FOR TODAY...

Be Your Own Best Friend

Everything changes and evolves. Even our relationships, including the one with ourselves. You may currently feel you're going through outside changes as well as inside ones and have been starting to look at certain friends or relationships differently. Perhaps you feel you have nothing in common anymore, or you just feel you've out-grown them, or they're really not treating you as you deserve. Don't fear this change as it's perfectly normal. Some people really do just come into our lives to teach us or to heal us for a period of time. Friendships or relationships shouldn't be such hard work or have you constantly questioning them. Once they're like this it's a sign that it's possibly time for you to move on. Don't feel you have to justify yourself to anyone. Just send the relationship love and ask the universe, God, Goddess or your spirit guides and angels (whoever you feel) to assist in cutting your invisible cords to detach you from a particular person, situation, and anything else which no longer serves a purpose in your life. Now is also the time to also be a better friend, to you! You do remember you don't you?...Start saying no to others a little more and yes to yourself. If you can't be your own best friend and really learn to love who you are then how can you truly be there for anyone else, supporting and loving others as you wish? Learn to always keep in check of your energy, coming from your heart as much as you can, so that you are able to feel stronger in yourself, feeling more prepared to be there for others and to see people and situations around you more clearly.

You're not obliged to keep anyone in your life you don't wish to, so never feel guilty about moving forward in whichever way you choose.

JUST FOR TODAY...

Spend Time With Mother Nature

Get outside and spend some quality time with Mother Nature (also known as Gaia) even if it's just five minutes in your garden. If the sunshine is out, let it shine down on your face so you can feel the warmth of its glow, or if the rain is falling, throw the umbrella away and let its cleansing waters trickle over your skin. Go on a long walk in the country and take in all the different sounds, smells, and sights. *Feel* the connection with the earth underneath your feet as you trek along, and be aware of every step. Just *be* and leave all your worries behind you. Maybe you're living in a busy city and are finding it hard to get to the countryside, if so, you could perhaps do some planting, or bring more plants inside your home. We all need the energy of the great Mother to help us feel that deeper bond with ourselves and the Earth. Walking amongst the trees and through the forests also makes us feel so good and raises our vibrational energy, it can help with depression and settle our breathing, slowing it down and steadying its flow.

So, get outside or bring the outside in…Mother Nature is calling you.

JUST FOR TODAY...

When The Feminine Heart Is Open

When we women open our hearts for ourselves, we also open our hearts for others

When the feminine heart is open *She* has the power to heal the greatest scars, empower the most fearful mind, and bring love to the loneliest soul.

When the feminine heart is open *Her* greatest strength emerges – Love…not only for others but for herself.
 Through Her opened heart, she helps open and Awaken the hearts of those around her; Women, Daughters, Men, and Sons.

When the feminine heart is open
Her true voice is spoken. Unafraid to share
her scars, inspiring others with her story,
and unapologetically herself.

When the feminine heart is open *Her*
greatest creations are birthed, her highest
intuition is awake, and her most beautiful
words are spoken.

When the feminine heart is open it is not
weakness you shall see, it is a wild warrior
who honours both her feminine and
masculine, the empowered goddess and
unleashed wolf.

When the feminine heart is open *She*
becomes a force of nature, at one with
Mother Earth and her great inner seasons of
emotions.

When the feminine heart is open
She honours her softness, but also her assertiveness, she opens herself to saying yes, but also knows when to say no, she unconditionally gives, but also allows herself to receive, and she never settles for anything or anyone who does not value her time or her worth.

When the feminine heart is open there is nothing more beautiful.

You see, this world *will* be saved by the Hearts of western woman, as it is only within the opened hearts of the feminine where the greatest healing power resides.

JUST FOR TODAY...

Express Your Playful Side

Sometimes we need to just let go of it all! Our inhibitions, our self-awareness, our fears about how we may seem to others, forget about work and forget about money and responsibilities, even if only for a short while. Your world won't fall apart if you choose to laugh and have fun! At times, we all need to step back, take a deep breath and realise just how short our life is. When we acknowledge this it helps us to release the pressure a little and surrender. The thing is, by allowing more time to enjoy life in any way you choose, you help yourself to think clearer, feel more positive, and pay more attention to what you need to do to get to where to want. This relaxed and carefree attitude will then attract the right people and situations into your life also. Look at it as a necessity rather than a luxury.

So go on, have a laugh, you might enjoy it!

JUST FOR TODAY...

Accept Yourself For All Which You Are

You are too hard on yourself at times when you really don't need to be. Remember to stop, breathe, and remember who you really are. Remind yourself;

- You *are* beautiful,
- You *can* do it,
- You *are* good enough,
- You *are* strong enough,
- You *are* brave enough,
- You *do* have the courage already to embrace your fears.

We are only human, we all hurt, bleed, feel and make many mistakes. No one is perfect, but this is what makes us human. If everyone was perfect we'd all be the same, and what's the fun in that?! It's our imperfections that give us our character and make us who we are. They're actually not really imperfections at all, they're just you. After all, what's imperfect to one person is perfect to someone else, what one person might dislike about you, another will embrace.

So accept yourself fully, because you are imperfectly perfect!

JUST FOR TODAY...

Live In Awe

When you next look at the world, try to imagine seeing things with the eyes of a child, forever intrigued, even with the smallest of things; a flower opening, a lady bird crawling, the web of a spider or the way our chest moves up and down whilst the air fills our lungs keeping us living. This message is to remind you to see more of this beauty in the world. From the moment you come into this world you are pure love with skin on. It's life that makes us anything else but love. Don't feel guilty about slowing down a little more to appreciate the moments, talking with a friend, listening to your children, going for a walk, reading a book, or just sitting in silence listening and being aware of all that's around you. There really is so much enchantment and beauty in the world. Once this is seen and felt in our hearts, it creates a warm glow in our soul, helping our light shine brighter and the life in our eyes to come alive!

JUST FOR TODAY...

Listen For The Signs

God, the Universe, Spirit, our Mother Gaia, the angels, are really trying to communicate with us at all times in many ways. Repetitive thoughts, feelings, or dreams, signs, even songs on the radio. They're also guiding you to *listen* for the hidden messages within others. Sometimes people can come across in an unwanted way and express anger, defensiveness, or rudeness, but this is really just a sign that there's more going on underneath then meets the eye. Remember to do your best to not take on others issues and lower energies as your own or as a personal attack on you. Try to develop more compassion for others and *feel* for them more. This doesn't mean you have to have them in your life or be there every time they call or are in need, or even try to solve all their problems, all this means is when someone 'pushes your buttons', showing them compassion or feeling compassion for them helps your energy stay loving. By not taking others personally and not being effected with their lower energy can help you give out a higher energy to them. Be more aware of your own feelings and thoughts. If you're reacting in a defensive or angry manor lately towards others, check in with your heart, asking for inner guidance to help you to see what's really going on inside you and *listen*. When people are angry or defensive, this is really just a less painful way of showing sadness, hurt, confusion, insecurity and pain. When these deep rooted things can be dealt with and understood, it clears the way for a more positive and happier way of feeling, which in turn will make your thoughts be more beautiful, whilst acting and responding with others in a better way also.

So listen, someone's trying to tell you something.

JUST FOR TODAY...

Release

Be aware of starting to release unwanted and past emotions now in any way you need. Go for a walk, cry, or speak to someone who's willing to listen. If you've been holding into unwanted feelings and emotions for far too long then now's the time to let go. Sometimes we hold on to feelings for longer than is needed as we can feel unresolved about certain people or situations. Sometimes we hold on to feelings as it helps us to feel in control (when really this isn't the case) and sometimes we hold on to old thought patterns and heavy feelings because we don't quite know how to let them go. Know that you are supported in this release. Trust in the universe to catch your unwanted, sad, angry, hurtful emotions whatever they may be, knowing it will give you strength and much needed healing for your heart and soul so you can start to move forward, feeling like a weights lifted, and beginning to see things clearer once again. All is well. Look up at the sky and breathe in life so you can wake up refreshed and cleansed. Tomorrow is a brand new day! Let what's gone be gone, and look forward to what's coming.

Release what no longer serves you, you are safe.

JUST FOR TODAY...

Honor Your Sensitivity

We women are born feelers, some of us more sensitive than others. When we experience energies and emotions at a high level it can overwhelm us, making us feel overcome with emotions. A message is being sent to you to remind you to honor your great sensitivity, even if at times you see it as a hindrance it's actually a blessing. Your ability to feel and pick up surrounding energies so strongly helps you to know what and who is good for your soul and also what is not. It helps you to be more empathetic and compassionate with others hearts and knowing how to help better.

You have been blessed with this gift from birth. Learn to love the way you just 'know' things and how great this truly is.

Cherish it always, it's there to lovingly guide you.

JUST FOR TODAY...

Remember Your 'Why'

Whatever it is you're doing or want to do or achieve, when you get nervous or start thinking "I can't" or "I'm not good enough", this is your ego talking and getting in the way of what's real. All you need to do is remember the reason *why* you're doing what you do or want to do and as long as your intention is for the greatest and highest good, focus on this and all will be amazing!

Keep asking "how may I serve?" and you will be guided to where you need, at the right time and the right place for all involved. All is happening exactly when it should, even if at the time you don't understand or see the reason, trust in the universe, trust in yourself and all that is love and peace and you'll find your way, helping others find their way too! Don't feel disheartened if you think others don't see the good in you or all the beautiful ways you help.

Mother Earth and Father sky see…this is all that matters.

JUST FOR TODAY...

Take The Leap

Don't rush, take it slow, when it's right, you will know.

When you are coming to the edge of your comfort zone at times you can find yourself fighting to resist moving forward in to the new, whatever it may be. Don't try to resist, just allow the natural flow of life to take you to where you need to be. Like a beautiful waterfall, cascading down to its next destination, without hesitation, just doing what it's meant to do. Step towards the edge and leap (metaphorically speaking!) when you let go and surrender like this, you'll find that things move more gracefully and peacefully. Others won't be able to help becoming captured by your 'no worry' attitude. This is not a time to fight, but surrender to spirit.

So deeply breathe and allow life's waterfall to carry you.

JUST FOR TODAY...

Speak Up! From The Heart

When *you* take a stand to say what you choose and say what you mean in every way, without confusion or hesitation, without holding a fear of what others will say or how others will respond, it liberates your soul by setting you free from insecurities. When you speak up you become a teacher to others who sometimes hold back. You help others to release their fears and doubts about using their *own* voice and encourages them to open up.

Speaking up can be a beautiful thing, as long as it's always done with kindness and love.

You will always come up against those who don't like your **strength at talking back** or speaking up, but let this be their issue, don't lose who *you* are and never compromise yourself to collude with the rest, always remain at your very best and speak the truth. You have this right, as we all do. You have a right to express your beliefs, ideas, opinions, happiness and grief as much as anyone.

Allowing another to belittle your voice or shame you says 'its ok, I don't mind', like you don't have a choice, but you do! and the more you keep quiet, the more others will control, making you give up who *you* are so that they can feel whole within themselves.

This doesn't seem right to me, everyone should feel free to express every part of who they are, but the only one who can truly break the silence and take that stand, is you.

So find that strength from deep within, find your true voice, and let old habits go so new ones can start to begin.

JUST FOR TODAY...

Purify Your Soul, Purify Your Space

Clear out and clean out!

Whether it's a walk in the rain, new surroundings, new healthier diet which involves much more water and less caffeine and sugars, spring cleaning your house which will help heal your soul, a warm relaxing bath with sea salts, or a good old chat and cry to help let go and release all that you've been holding onto, even parting with those not good for you. Unfortunately we sometimes have to let go of others who are bringing us down, but once you start on this new cleansing path, your thoughts will start to shift into more purer, focused and more positive ways of thinking and in turn help you *feel* more content and happy with life and your precious journey.

So do what you have to do. Let go of what's old and holding you back so you can embrace what's new to help you move forward!

JUST FOR TODAY...

Remember Who You Are

Do not deny your greatness and the strength you have. Certain situations call for you to use this so that it builds up within your soul. Once this is done, no external behaviors or situations will affect you and you'll start focusing on the future instead of the past, looking at your strengths instead of your weaknesses and seeing things with clarity instead of through the fog. If you've been losing who you are and allowing your mind to jump and becoming unsettled, gain that control within your heart once again. Imagine yourself as a tower of strength, grounded in the earth with your head held high. Remember that you can't control others behaviors, how others see you, or what others may say about you, past, present and future, but you can control yourself, your words, your actions, and most of all how you see yourself, which is all that really matters.

Stand proud and steady as a rock while the world goes on around you. You're going to be fine. Remember who you are, where you've been, what you've been through and where you're going. Use that as your strength. It doesn't matter if others don't see it, all that matters is that you do.

Keep strong!

JUST FOR TODAY...

Take Time To Breathe!

Stop for a moment and just breathe. That's all you need to do. Feel the breath filling your lungs and feel it coming out again. Be thankful for every breath, as without it you wouldn't be here! Take a walk in the woods, fields, and country lanes so you can be at one with nature. The trees breathe out oxygen which we then take in, and we breathe out carbon dioxide which the trees then take in, it's because of this reason we feel so good after a brisk walk outside. When your breathing has been too shallow, over time this can start effecting you in many ways such as stress, anxiety, or over thinking.

So take time out from everyone, from work, from people, from kids etc., meditate if you like (even though you don't need to meditate to just be and breathe) this can help you focus more deeply on yourself and your thoughts.

Once you correct your breathing things will start feeling more balanced emotionally and you'll be able to get back to *you* once again.

JUST FOR TODAY...

Allow Your Spirit Rest So It May Grow

Have faith in your spiritual journey even in times of suffering, stillness, and pain. Trust that all is happening as it should and allow this process to happen naturally. Don't try to force this spiritual growth, it is already occurring in every moment. Like the lotus flower which comes out and blossoms in the day then retreats back into the muddy waters at night to get its much needed rest and nutrients, you too need that rest. Whether it be from others, the world, or even yourself, but we sometimes don't know this, so life takes over.

If you feel as if things have come to a halt or you're in the darkness, be patient, have faith, trust, and allow. This is exactly what's needed. You are supported by spirit and loved unconditionally.

Your spiritual unfoldment is always occurring!

All *will* be well!

JUST FOR TODAY...

Embrace New Beginnings

New amazing beginnings are always just around the corner, awaiting to happen for you, always remember this! Embrace every single moment with an open heart as there is only peace, love, and Joy ahead for you. New beginnings and changes can sometimes feel scary, but this doesn't mean their wrong.

'Are you acting to the present, or re-acting to the past?'

We can sometimes get so caught up in what's been, with thoughts of last year, last week, or even earlier in our day. We can go over conversations thinking about what someone said earlier, what we should have said in reply, what happened last year, or what we have to do tomorrow, leaving us feeling exhausted and unfocused! All this really does though is stop us from fully enjoying what's going on now and the great opportunities that lie ahead of us.

We hold onto too much fear of what's been before, how others have treated us badly, the outcome of old situations etc...The list goes on!

Let it go...

Don't allow your past to manifest in to your future. You're safe, loved, and free to be whoever you choose!

So when you look forward, do it with a smile and let today be the beginning of the rest of your life.

JUST FOR TODAY...

Remember Your Innocence

When we were young, we all made mistakes, we all said or done things that were wrong, but we didn't beat ourselves up too much, as we were learning. Why when we become adult's does society, as well as ourselves, punish us so much for our mistakes? We may be adults, but we're only human. People say that you can forgive someone once as that was probably a 'mistake' but two or three times is wrong. I truly believe that sometimes we have to mess up more than once so we can be fully aware of a situation, how it made us feel, or how it made others feel. If we don't mess up and make these mistakes, then how do we know if their wrong or not? We can't just rely on what others tell us, we have to know for ourselves. It's the pain from this learning that teaches us which makes us wiser and stronger in the long run, if we let it. The thing is, we can all judge, but until we are in a person's situation, we really have no understanding of why someone does what they do, speaks how they speak or thinks how they think. We are not born bad, we just do or say bad things at times. I don't think it matters how long it takes someone to learn from their mistakes, as long as they do eventually learn. I'm still learning from certain mistakes I've made, but I'm aware, not because someone's told me to be, but because I've realised things myself, which is the first step to any change.

Remind yourself of this innocence you have, we all have, even as adults; no-ones perfect, so don't be too hard on yourself. Let go of the guilt and fear and just say "ok, I've messed up, (for the second, third of forth time!!) But I am going to try my hardest to do better next time". That's all anyone can do.

So return to your innocence and Learn to laugh at yourself more. After all, you are a child of Father God and Mother Goddess, so allow yourself to be that.

JUST FOR TODAY...

Keep Moving

Learning to have trust and faith in our journey is one of the greatest and most peaceful things you can do for your soul. Its surrendering but in a good, empowering way, saying 'I've done all I can, it's up to you now God'. When we get to a point in our life where we just can see how something is going to unfold, it's like a bend in the river with the sun shining around the corner, we can see the light but nothing else, not seeing or knowing exactly what's ahead. Keep moving.

Just like the sunshine which beams down upon the rivers bend, amazing beautiful things await you also. Go with life's flow, don't try to resist. There will be signs along the way showing you which way to turn. So just breathe, relax, and let the river of life carry you.

JUST FOR TODAY...

Don't Allow Those Heavy People To Put Out Your Light

Shine!

Others may try to put out your light but don't let them! No matter how they are with you, how they criticize or how they judge, just keep being you! By staying true to yourself, the light you radiate will either turn the darkness of others away or help them shine with you so you can shine together.

A beautiful little quote about 'those haters' from Maya Angelou is;

"Baby, those people can't hold a candle to the light God already has shining on your face"

I absolutely love this! Something I now like to say to others who are struggling with dealing with those 'heavy people'.

Take time to smile more whilst telling yourself 'I *am* beautiful, I *am* happy and content, I *am* wonderful just how I am, I *do* deserve happiness, I *am* worthy, I *am* enough! Get out doors and let the sun shine beam down on you, reminding you of its warmth and reminding you that this is how you make others feel when you stay true to you and continue to shine the great light you were born with.

JUST FOR TODAY...

Emerge From Your Cocoon

Life sometimes takes an unexpected turn, giving you no choice but to go through intense changes. Even if you are struggling, these changes are much needed, so be aware of 'going with the flow' instead of trying to resist. Most changes happen slowly and gradually, but not always. You need to surrender to this so you can fully let go of who you are and how your life's been so you can embrace your brand new life and 'emerge' into the new you. Don't think you're unprepared, you're not. Have faith that things will work out. It may not be what you expected, but it's what you need. This is also a time to adjust your thinking about others, yourself, and life. Just like a dragonfly, spends years living as what's known as a 'nymph' then one day transforms into a beautiful colorful dragonfly with a new purpose, a new life, and a new body, never looking back or being able to go back to what it once was. These changes are a beautiful and natural thing for you. Embrace them fully!

JUST FOR TODAY...

Be Proud Of How Far You've Came

Celebrate!

Plain and simple. For all your achievements, recent and old, or anything you've pulled yourself through and become stronger from or let go of. You have a right to be proud and remind yourself how much you've accomplished, whilst also feeling proud to show others. There's absolutely nothing wrong or 'big headed' (as some might think) with telling others how proud you feel of yourself once in a while. If others don't want to celebrate with you, that's ok. It can be hard to see someone doing well if our own lives are falling apart so try not to take it personally. If you feel there's no one around to listen or who wants to listen, just keep your heart beaming from the inside out, being proud doesn't always have to be an external thing, it can be a quietly hidden smile within our hearts, a knowing internally of how far we've come, helping us to feel grateful for where we are in life with a beautiful bounce in our step.

It doesn't matter if others don't share how proud they are of you, all that matters is that you feel proud of yourself and the amazing woman you have now become.

Well done to you!

JUST FOR TODAY...

I SEE You

I SEE how you try, your great courage, your struggles, your tears, and your pain.

I SEE your great determination to never give up, even when you feel you're standing alone.

I SEE your strength to create your own path and the loneliness that can also come from this.

I SEE your clarity, your confusion, your passion, and also your doubt.

I SEE how you give so much of your heart to others.

I SEE your deep compassion, empathy, and understanding to all humans, because you've been through the challenges.

I SEE how you continue to shine your light so you can light the way for others.

Through all the pain, the mistakes, and the struggles, I SEE your spirit, your divine nature, your heart, your beauty, and the truth of your soul, even when you don't see it yourself.

So never stop believing in the greatness which you are and all that you can become.

I SEE you, and you are beautiful!

JUST FOR TODAY...

Stop Procrastinating

Now's the time to do more of what you love. If you've been feeling quite lethargic, mentally and physically, this is down to not doing enough of what you enjoy, and the less we do these things, the harder it can be to get into them again and we start to become lazy. Think of what you really love and the things you want to achieve. What gives you a warm glow or puts a smile on your face? What gives your heart and soul passion? What have you always thought about doing but keep putting off? What goes through your mind the most about getting done or completing? An incredible contentment fills us when we make commitments, either personal or to others, and stick to them. If there are things you've been longing to do or achieve for yourself, be prepared to let go of being there for others for a while, but don't feel guilty about this. Once we focus on making our own goals happen instead on focusing on others, great things start happening in *our* lives and we feel a purpose and belonging which makes us feel happier, more content within, more content with life, and helps us to become much better individuals for ourselves and those around us.

So don't keep leaving things until tomorrow, stop making excuses, and just do it! You'll feel much better once you make those first steps.

JUST FOR TODAY…

Nurture Your Soul

Being a kind, caring, loving, and nurturing person by nature can be hard at times. You're kind to all, big or small, animals, plants, oceans, trees etc. You're good at helping others to realise *their* full potential and to learn to love themselves more, you have a 'knack' for *feeling* and just *knowing* what's going on inside others hearts and who they really are, but many times are unable to do this for yourself. Because of this intuitiveness you have, you're a born healer! Remind yourself of this, but also be aware that you need to be giving what you give to others to yourself a bit more. You don't need to be so strong all of the time. It's ok to show your vulnerable side once in a while and let others be there for *you*.

Nurture, love, and care for *your* needs as much as you do for others. Trust your great intuition more. Your spot on when it comes to knowing what's right for everyone else but you doubt what's right when it comes to you. Don't!

JUST FOR TODAY...

Stand Your Ground

Standing up for your beliefs, who you are, and what you stand for, shows others that you're important too, whilst also showing respect for yourself. Some people say 'to get respect you have to give respect', personally, I disagree with this a little, my experiences have shown me that just because you have respect for yourself and give this to another, does not mean you will get it back. Respect has to be a two way thing, *both* people have to have it before they can give it to one another.

Not everyone will respect you for standing your ground, but try not to focus on these people as their actions say more about them then you. The important thing is that *you* will gain a greater respect for yourself, helping to raise *your* self-worth and inner strength.

Speaking up doesn't have to be done nastily or in a negative way, it is possible to be both loving and strong simultaneously, whilst also getting your message across. Leaving things unsaid or allowing another to overpower your voice can make things fester, which is never a good thing for either person. I want to remind you to stand up for your beliefs and be true to who you are.

You *are* strong enough. You *are* important.

JUST FOR TODAY...

Say No!

Some people think saying no is easy, but it's actually one of the hardest things to say, for fear of confrontation, fear of letting someone down or fear of not being liked or accepted. But it takes a lot more strength to say *no* to someone then to go along with what they want. Saying no doesn't mean you're selfish or a horrible person, it just means you're valuing your own needs and making yourself important to, which you are. Of course there could be a number of reasons why you're saying no. Whatever they may be, don't feel you need to justify yourself. It's *your* choice, your prerogative, and at the times that you do say yes, make sure you're doing it because you want to, or out of the kindness of your own heart. If you do something with, or for someone halfheartedly, you're not being true to them or yourself, and in the long run will only find yourself becoming resentful of them for giving your time when you really didn't want to.

As long as you respect others right to say no and allow them to feel ok with not fulfilling your needs all the time, then feel free to say no to whoever you wish, whenever you wish, without feeling bad and without feeling guilty. This is *your* life. Live it how you wish and never feel afraid to just say no.

JUST FOR TODAY...

See The Lesson Through The Pain

Constant strength doesn't exist. It's just like everything else in life, you have to work on it every day to keep it flowing. This might sound disheartening to you, or it might sound like a weight lifted. Being truly strong isn't about those times that you actually are, it's the times when you're falling but know how to pick yourself up and carry on. I believe myself to be a pretty balanced and awakened woman, but have had to (and still do) put a lot of work into becoming this way. Even so, I still have moments/days, where I lose that strength and that happiness, I shout, I argue, I swear, I lose my faith, I doubt who I am and what I do etc., but it's in *these* moments I've had to make myself stronger than ever. It's in *these* moments I've had to do my best to find the positive in life still. It's in *these* moments I've had to try my hardest to find that happiness again an come back to my heart.

If you can find that glimmer of hope in your lowest of times, *that's* where you'll find your *true* strength.

Just remember, next time your struggling, don't be too hard on yourself. Even the most balanced and spiritual of us still fall. We have to, so we can learn to pick ourselves up again. We all have choices. We can either chose to be a victim, or not, to stay stuck or to keep moving. It really is as simple as that. Don't think "why me?!" when bad things happen. Appreciate Gods giving you a chance to learn. If we ask God for strength he doesn't give us strength, he gives us opportunities to prove to ourselves how strong we really are, and the more opportunities we have, the stronger we can grow…if we chose to.

JUST FOR TODAY…

Create Harmony Through Balance

Everything in life is about balance. It's the natural flow. With the downs comes the ups, and vice versa, even though at times we wish it had more ups and living was a constant state of peace. The thing is, we can all find more peace, regardless of what the world brings, but it has to come from within. We first need to accept the world for what it is-then let things be or make necessary changes. When the chaos goes on around us, be it life, or people, it's simply a matter of shifting our internal dialog into more positive thoughts and directing our energy to ourselves, our goals, our future, and the positive things to come, as energy flows where attention goes! A message reminding you that now's the time to return to your inner sanctuary, breathe, and allow your breath to guide you to a peaceful and loving place that resides in your heart...

Only a peaceful heart within, brings peace without. Truly becoming a Priestess of yourself is being able to keep this internal peace, even amongst the chaos.

JUST FOR TODAY...

Give

Wanting, needing, and desiring, are all very human and very normal things we all feel, but what about giving?

It truly is a beautiful thing to give without expecting anything in return. It does something amazing to your soul, to your heart, and to your energy, something which I could tell you about, but until you actually *give* this way it's not a feeling that can be fully understood. Great inner peace, courage, and strength, is made from selflessly giving with all our hearts. Whether we get it back from the one we gave to or not, *all* good deeds come back eventually, even if our good deed comes back in the form of inner peace, this should be enough, as peace is something which can be very hard to attain so we should feel very grateful when it comes.

When people think of giving, what usually springs to mind is something like money or material things, but giving is so much more than that! Time… Time is the best thing you can give to another, especially in this day and age with all the internet interactions, the iPhone, iPad and fb etc. where people seem to be interacting less face to face. It's actually so easy but so beautiful to just stop and give someone a little of your undivided and uninterrupted attention, be it an ear to listen, a shoulder to cry on, an encouraging word, or a hand to hold. A piece of your heart given and lovingly placed into another's is the most beautiful thing you could ever give.

JUST FOR TODAY...

Deeply Empathize

To see what another sees, to try and feel what another feels, to understand what another understands, to hurt, to grieve, and to love like another, this is empathising. We may never fully *know* exactly what's going on inside someone else's heart, but we can *all* try to if we really want.

We literally have to think 'what if that was me? What would *I* want someone to say? How would *I* want to be heard?'

Step into someone's soul, long enough to feel their heart, deep enough to taste their tears, and be kind enough to say 'I'm here with understanding and without judgment,

I'm here'. Sometimes, that's all someone needs.

JUST FOR TODAY...

Ignore The Noise

When we connect with our spirit it becomes easier to dis-connect from anything which does not serve us well. By journeying deeper *within* we can pull further away from all that is *without* and go to a peaceful, quiet, and almost meditative state of being. Pure bliss!

Whether you work in the country or in a busy city, once you learn to find that inner sanctuary, the noise of the world or even of your own thoughts will be easier to turn down, a little like a volume switch on the radio.

The downside to this is that the more you venture into this quiet space, the louder the noise from the world can seem, but don't let that put you off from going on this 'silent journey' for it is one of the greatest things you will do for yourself for many reasons.

It will help to keep you balanced, it will assist in shutting out the mental noise your mind may want to make, it will bring a great amount of peace, and it will even help shut out those moments when your children are driving you a little mad! Can't be bad!

So if you really want to ignore the noise, journey within, where all becomes still, and the silence has room to unfold.

JUST FOR TODAY...

Show Compassion

This can be one of the hardest things to do, especially when someone's hurt us or wronged us in some way, but showing compassion isn't about still being there for another who's treated you poorly or allowing them back in your life, it's just a way of saying 'I understand why you are like you are and my heart feels for you, I wish you weren't hurting' etc., or something along those lines, and sending out heart felt love to them with your energy. This may never change how the person is, as change is an internal thing which has to be done with an awareness of self, but what it *will* do is stop any lower or hurtful energy from still accumulating, helping to keep *your* energy high and loving which is the most important thing.

Showing compassion comes from first realising that how another is has nothing to do with you and should not be taken personally, it's just an internal battle they are struggling with within themselves.

Compassion is just noticing the human struggles in all of us and whether right or wrong or some actions worse than others, it's seeing that we *all* deserve to be heard and understood, even if not accepted.

JUST FOR TODAY...

Do Not Anger

Anger can hurt many people who are on the tail end of it, but like most actions we take, in the long run it will do more harm to *us* and how *we* feel within ourselves.

Have you ever noticed that the word anger is only one letter short or danger?!

When we get angry, especially towards another, we are actually losing all of our control, our self-respect, and our dignity, lowering our energy and making us feel exhausted afterwards whilst also a little regretful.

If you feel yourself getting angry, raising your voice, or about to say something which you may regret later, remind yourself to breathe, then walk away! Sometimes, when we know what we are going to say or do next will be more harmful than not, it's best to leave the situation, calm your energy down, give your throat a little loving healing and regain focus. Perhaps ask yourself 'why am I getting so angry?' or 'why am I allowing this other person's words to hurt me so much?' What you'll realise by taking this little break is that how another is has more to do with them than you, and that when we get angry it's just a less hurtful way of expressing our sadness or pain. I believe the angrier a person is the more pain they are trying to cover up. When you can learn to truly accept why you are feeling how you are and express this in a more calmer and truthful way, you will feel enormously empowered and much more in control.

It doesn't matter how the other person may respond, all that matters is how *you* do.

JUST FOR TODAY...

Cry

The reason we feel much better after a good cry is because around 10% of our tears are water and the other 90% is emotion, so when you're blubbering away just think of all those pent up feelings you're releasing!

Even though I'm a very sensitive woman, at times I can find it extremely hard to cry for certain things, so what I do in these cases is get cozy, get a cup of herbal tea, put a good film on which I know will be sad or happy-sad and cry my little eyes out! We can have so many thoughts, feelings, and emotions running through our head, our heart, and our soul, that we don't always know where to start or how to shift them, but once we start the process of releasing these emotions we've held onto, our thoughts 'de-clutter' and we actually start to feel more focused within ourselves and our journey.

Your tears don't always have to be of sadness, they can be tears of joy! At times even our happiness can become overwhelming, and like all emotions it needs to be released also.

Some of us can find it really hard to let go like this in front of others, personally I don't feel this to be wrong or right, I feel that as long as you let it out and feel better for it, then you just go ahead and let it out wherever and whenever you feel comfortable!

JUST FOR TODAY...

Paint Your Feelings

Some of us can struggle to express our enormous range of feelings by talking, in this case, it's good if you can express this in a creative way. More often than not, people think that a painting needs to be a great work of art or you need to be a top artist, but this just isn't true. Art can be anything you want, and what makes art beautiful, is when it its unique, and it's only unique when it comes from within you.

Painting or drawing can be as small or as big as you want. Don't think about it too much or your art will be something which comes from your head instead of your heart, and it's only when we work from our heart and soul that the truth comes to the surface.

Through painting you can begin to visualize on canvas what you've been holding onto or how you truly feel, it's only when we start to become aware of ourselves like this and discover just how deep our soul travels is when our healing journey begins.

JUST FOR TODAY...

Find Your True Nature

Your true nature is who you are when you're by yourself, who you are when you are with those people who you love the most and feel comfortable with and who you are when no one's watching.

Inside, we all know who we are or who we want to be, but more often than not we hold ourselves back because of the fear of how we may be perceived by others. We worry of judgment, criticism, and not being accepted, but when you truly accept yourself, even you're not so great points, you worry less about being accepted from others.

One thing I've noticed in life is that it doesn't matter how nice your are, not everyone is going to like you or connect with your spirit, so one day a long time ago now, I thought 'well if not everyone's going to like me anyway, I may as well just be myself, whoever that is'. It was one of the most liberating things I done. To actually get to a point when I wasn't 'thinking' of who I was being and just 'being' it. I realised overtime that it takes much less energy to show our true nature than it does to 'pretend' to be somebody else.

Being this way also gives others encouragement to do the same. Seeing someone who is totally at ease with who they are and showing this to the world helps others to release their own fears about being themselves also.

JUST FOR TODAY...

Be Like Water

There is no greater medicine or more natural flow in this world than water. Every living thing needs it to survive. It literally keeps us going.

Water is also a great survivor on its own. It can carve its way, even through the greatest of storms, and when trapped, it just makes a new path. The thing is, when troubles arise in our life and suffering takes over, whether we think we can conquer or whether we think we cannot, we'll be right.

Take yourself to a beautiful river, lake, or even to the beach, and watch the water. Watch how incredible it is, watch how peacefully it flows, but reminding yourself that even through the peacefulness which water can bring, it can also bring great strength, but mostly, it just flows. No one can stop it, even if they tried, it would take some doing and eventually would most likely find the tiniest of cracks to make its way through.

What I want you to do is to become one with the water. Hear its flow, touch it with your hands or bare feet and feel the calm it brings, connect with the waters spirit then take that with you wherever you go. *Know* that however hard things are in your life, you too can make a choice to keep moving forward, making your own paths, and flowing peacefully in your *own* way.

Just like water.

JUST FOR TODAY...

Watch Who You're Comparing Yourself To

We all compare, to a degree, it's pretty normal, buts what's important is *who* we are comparing ourselves to. We often look around at the 'best bits' of others' lives and either wish for the same or think they have it better, when what we should be doing is finding our *own* true passion, our *own* happiness and seeing all the beauty which we *have* created rather than what we have not. None of us truly know what another's life is about, the reason we get so insecure is because we compare our 'behind the scenes reel' with others 'highlights reel', seeing only the 'good bits', but I can guarantee that if you looked further, their life wouldn't be so different than yours, it may even be worse! Of course there are those who have more money, but money doesn't always bring happiness. I used to be guilty of this, wishing for the lives of others instead of my own, but when I finally got to look up close to these 'perfect but not so perfect' lives, I realised just how wrong I was, which made me then see the beauty of all I truly had, which then helped me start putting energy into creating the life I desired. Occasionally I find myself looking up to certain very successful people, this I find is ok as there are people out their which do inspire me to do better and 'up my game'.

There may always be someone somewhere who has it better, but there's also millions around the world who don't and probably never will. A very long time ago I made a promise to myself to never compare to another, and if I ever *do* find my mind going to that place, I compare myself and my life to the person I was yesterday, always trying to improve, I also think of those less fortunate and have learnt to feel extremely grateful for all that I *do* have rather than all I don't.

When you learn to see the beauty in your own life and work at making it more beautiful, you'll never worry about comparing yourself to another again.

JUST FOR TODAY...

Pass It On

If someone shows you kindness, pass it on.
If someone kisses your cheek, pass it on.
If someone lends you a hand, pass it on.
If someone gives you a hug, pass it on.
If someone speaks a kind word, pass it on.
If someone builds you up, pass it on.
If someone shows forgiveness, pass it on.
If someone says 'I love you', pass it on.
If someone does a good deed for you, pass it on.

We all have the ability to help another, and even though we can't help everyone, everyone can help someone.

So do a good deed, spread the seed of love so that it may be passed on throughout the world.

Everyone's heart can be touched if we all learn to pass it on.

JUST FOR TODAY...

Stay Positive

Refuse to complain, criticize, or condemn anyone or anything.

If someone's name comes up which you may not quite like, don't say a word. If the dinners ruined, just throw it away and chow down on beans on toast! If people are trying to put their heavy energies on you, smile, keep positive and let it go. If the bills need paying, if your kids haven't cleaned their room, if your partner hasn't kept to taking the bin out! Whatever it may be, keep your mouth closed and give love and positivity anyway. Talk about your joys rather than your struggles. Express your love rather than your hurt. Give thanks to all you *do* receive.

You can't help if another is not so positive with you, but you *can* choose not to respond to it. Think of all the beautiful and great things entering your life or those which are in your life already, and whatever happens, if you haven't got something nice to say, don't say anything at all!

JUST FOR TODAY...

Give Yourself Room To Blossom

Remind your heart that it's ok to need space, be it away from family, friends, your partner or your kids.

It's ok to get away from it all, on your own, to travel to a place where you can truly forget about everything and everyone but yourself. It can be hard to bloom, to grow, and to find who we are when we are constantly surrounded by other energies that are possibly bringing us down or demanding our attention. Don't feel guilty with wanting space for yourself and don't feel guilty about the length of time you need. There is no time limit for your healing journey, it takes as long as it takes to feel your wonderful self again, to return to the strong courageous woman that you are and to be able to walk back into your life with a knowing that you can now handle anything, with love and peace in your heart and soul.

So allow yourself room to breathe, room to grow, and room to blossom into the beautiful rose you we're born to be.

JUST FOR TODAY...

Be Like Wood

When I say this, I want you to connect with the trees. I want you to acknowledge the incredible strength and wisdom that comes from these beautiful earth creations.

When you think of a tree, any tree, how does it make you feel? What vision do you get? Where in your soul does the energy resonate?

When most people think of trees, they think words like- *majestic, wise, healing, strong, powerful, mother nature, oxygen, beauty, rooted, grounded, earth, knowledge...* The list goes on, but do you see the beautiful pattern and the energy that they give off?

I want you, in your own time, to go out and make this connection with the trees (even if it's just one particular tree). No matter how big or small, just like us, everything wants to be noticed and appreciated.

Once you feel you've made that connection, take that feeling into your heart. *Be* the tree, watch how it sways and moves beautifully in the wind, try to re-create these movements yourself. I know it can be hard or embarrassing for some to move their body in this way, but trust me, you *will* feel better for it. Be like a child. A child doesn't focus on if others are watching or if their doing it right, they just get lost in their own little precious movements.

Put some beautiful music on if it helps and be conscious to make each movement slow, soft, and flowing, but also keeping a part of your focus on being grounded and as rooted to the earth as a sacred tree.

Connecting in this way with these majestic woodland creatures will help give an incredibly empowering whoosh of emotions running through your very core, helping you to forever stay strong in who you are,

Always.

JUST FOR TODAY...

Don't Allow

Don't allow the cruelness of the world to make you hard.

Don't allow the hate to keep you from loving.

Don't allow the pain to steal your joy.

Don't allow the chaos to take away your peace.

Don't allow another's voice to quieten your own.

Don't allow old habits to stop you from making new ones.

Don't allow the bitterness of yesterday to steal the sweetness of today.

Don't allow who you were to stop you becoming who you wish to be.

Don't allow someone else's 'cants' stop *your* 'cans'.

and don't allow into your life, your heart, your spirit and your soul, anything or anyone which may try to stop you seeing all the beauty which is within you, which surrounds you, and which can be a part of your life.

Living in the knowledge that even if others can't see it, *you* will always choose to see the magnificent light which lies in everything and everyone.

JUST FOR TODAY...

Stop Saying Sorry

Sorry is a funny word to me. It isn't said enough when it should be, then said loads when it really doesn't need to be!

There are many times when we should say sorry, but only if there's true meaning behind it, then there are times when saying sorry can become a habit. It's all about being assertive but in a positive and kind way.

If you're looking for permission, then I'm giving you the permission to stop! Right now!

Sometimes we say sorry when it really isn't our fault, or we say sorry because we've said something which someone else has interpreted as wrong. Why should you say sorry for just being yourself?

Obviously, if you're being mean, hurtful, or nasty, then it's nice to apologize, but if you're just giving an opinion and talking from *your* heart, then carry on. Put yourself in check and close your mouth before the word 'sorry' passes your lips. You don't have to say sorry for everything.

Many people I meet say sorry for not answering their phone, sorry for being a few minutes late, sorry when someone else bumps into *them*! These are just a few examples, but do you see know how the word 'sorry' can be used when we really don't need to?

Even so, sorry can be a beautiful word when it's really needed, when it's meant and when the thing you're saying sorry for isn't repeated, this takes a lot of strength, but it also takes a lot of strength to be assertive within yourself and know when there really is no need to apologize at all.

JUST FOR TODAY...

Value love

Love is many different things which comes in many different forms. What love means to one person may be different to another. Each is ok. There is no right and wrong way.

To me, love is all things kind. Love is giving to another in millions of small or big ways, often or not so often, making someone else smile and feel appreciated or acknowledged for the beautifully human they are. Love is making someone feel happy in your company, love is being honest, love is appreciating and accepting someone fully and being true to them, even behind their back, and love is seeing all the beauty and greatness within another even when they can't see it themselves. But this is just *my* outlook on love.

I've learnt over the years that we all give love in such different ways, yet if we don't take time to realise these differences, we can think or feel another doesn't care or doesn't love us enough if they aren't giving how *we* give, but this isn't true. I don't care to reason or question anymore why people give in the many different ways they do, I've just learnt to accept it.

Over-all, love is one of the greatest feelings and life's most precious gift, whether you're giving it or receiving it, so value it in every single beautiful and unique way it comes.

JUST FOR TODAY...

Don't Hurt, Just Love

Don't hurt for the ones that aren't there, just love the ones that are.

Don't hurt for the opportunities you missed, just love the ones you took.

Don't hurt for those who have passed, just love the memories you made.

Don't hurt for all you haven't got, just love all that you have.

Don't hurt for those mistakes you made, just love the ones you got right.

Don't hurt for those harsh words, just love the words which made you smile. But, most importantly…

Don't hurt for all that you are not, just LOVE *all* that you are!

JUST FOR TODAY...

Harvest Your Heart

Put your hand on your heart, right now, and tell her you love her. Tell her you're sorry for holding onto all of that hurt and grief. Tell her you forgive her for all those foolish mistakes she made. Tell her to let go of the guilt. Tell her she's safe to love. Remind her just how amazing she is. Tell her 'thank you' for all those beautiful heartfelt moments, 'thank you' for how much she's gave even though she may not have always got it back, 'thank you' for having the strength to walk away from anyone who was bad for her soul, whether it be friend, lover, job, acquaintance or family, 'thank you' for her compassion, her empathy and her understanding, 'thank you' for her gratitude, for her love, for her peace and for still beating so strongly after every single emotion she has had to carry throughout life.

Feel her beating. She's beating for you. She's keeping your body strong.

She is truly incredible!

Wake up every morning with renewed gratitude at how she still beats for another day. Be gentle with her, listen to her, protect her, and harvest her thoroughly throughout the year so that new seeds can blossom beautifully with love.

JUST FOR TODAY...

Wherever you go, whatever you do,
Not just today but all year through,
Give all of your heart, all that is true,
All that is real, all that is you.

About the Author

Gaia Rose –

The Awakened Woman®, author of 'In My Heart I Know', is becoming one of the most admired UK Spiritual teachers, inspirational speakers, and authors, due to her down-to-earth nature, her wide open heart, her incredible story, and her unmistakable voice!

She is a force of Nature, a Wild, Free-Spirited Awakened Woman of the world who creates her own rules, encouraging others to do the same, stirring the inner magic within every heart that crosses her path.

Gaia is available for book signings and speaking engagements worldwide.

For all bookings and enquiries please contact:

info@gaiarose.co.uk.

Keep connected with Gaia;
Website – www.gaiarose.co.uk
Facebook – GaiaRoseOfficial
Instagram – Gaia__Rose